A LIFE FOR GOD IN INDIA

A LIFE FOR GOD IN INDIA

MEMORIALS OF MRS JENNIE FULLER OF AKOLA AND BOMBAY

HELEN S. DYER

GYAN

Published by

Gyan Publishing House
5, Ansari Road
Daryaganj, New Delhi-110002
Phone: 011-47034999, 9811692060
E-mail: books@gyanbooks.com

Distribution Network
gyanbooks.com
India, USA, Canada, UK, Australia

ISBN: 978-93-6780-059-1 (HB)

First Published, 1903

2nd Impression 2024

Printed at: Gyan Press, Delhi.

A LIFE FOR GOD IN INDIA: MEMORIALS OF MRS JENNIE FULLER OF AKOLA AND BOMBAY

Author: HELEN S. DYER

A Life for God in India

Yrs in His service
Jennie Fuller

A Life for God in India

Memorials of Mrs Jennie Fuller of Akola and Bombay

By

Helen S. Dyer

Author of

Pandita Ramabai; the Story of her Life; &c.

New York Chicago Toronto

Fleming H. Revell Company

London Edinburgh

TABLE OF CONTENTS

CHAPTER IX

CHAPTER X

CHAPTER XI

CHAPTER XII

APPENDIX

INTRODUCTORY

THIS little book does not claim to be a biography. It is but a simple attempt to gather up the threads of a life lived for God, and to show how He glorified Himself thereby. It claims to show how a life offered, consecrated, and accepted for the King's service, fitted into His plans for mission work in India, and became a factor in the extension of the knowledge of God over an entire province. It claims to show also how God used this life to edify and extend His Church on earth, and to lift individual Christian souls into higher aims of service; to inspire the home churches with missionary zeal, and rouse them to a sense of their responsibility in regard to prayer for missions.

Our subject, Mrs Jennie Fuller, was a living, loving personality, who gave out to others as freely as God gave to her. In discussing a missionary biography with a literary friend a few weeks before the close of her life on earth, Mrs Fuller remarked, "No one can write a biography of me when I am gone. I have kept no diary, and my letters for several years have been but notes, except to my children." But though Mrs Fuller kept no diary and wrote few letters, she had for some years realised that God had given her many experiences of His love and favour, that she might give them out to others. She loved to magnify His name with her pen, and thus, perhaps unconsciously to herself, she wrote much of her own life story. She loved hard lessons in order that she might thereby be qualified to teach others, and she rejoiced to pass on sweet thoughts that God gave her. From various sources these have been collected, and in this book, it may be said, "She being dead, yet speaketh."

"HER HUSBAND ALSO, AND HE PRAISETH HER."

In supplying a few notes and connecting links for this story, Mr Fuller puts a good testimony on record concerning her. He writes: "I realise that Mrs Fuller's life was a very precious legacy for her children and for all of us who knew her. There was so much of God in it. He did much for and in her, and that made it possible for Him to do much through her. There were the years of quiet toil before we joined the Alliance when she was so hungry to know the fulness of the Spirit, and even then there was a measure of the Spirit which made her a blessing to many. But God saw the deep desire to know Him, and in a remarkable degree He granted that desire. She was so genuine, and longed to *be* rather than *appear to be* filled with the Spirit. She had unusual natural gifts which she so fully gave to God that He could use them for His glory.

"The depth and strength of her convictions and her sincere purpose to be true to all the light which God had given her were very noticeable points in her character. She was one of the truest souls I have ever known. She was a woman of prayer, and when she felt clear in her guidance her opinions were of great value. When perplexed over matters, she would wait on God for weeks for light, and when she found it she had a gift of imparting it to others. She had by nature unusual gifts as a teacher, and these gifts were consecrated to God and illuminated and intensified by the indwelling of the Holy Spirit. God often helped her to make truth very plain to the simple native Christians by illustrations and incidents.

"She loved her friends very deeply, and naturally longed to please them, but her loyalty to Christ made her very faithful in dealing with them, and she was willing to be misunderstood or even for a time to forfeit a friend's approval rather than be disloyal to Christ and the truth which He had made plain to her. I lived with her for nineteen years, and as I look back over those years I realise that God gave me for a wife one of the best women I have ever known."

Testimonies of others of her friends have been gathered into the Appendix, which will be found not the least interesting and inspiring portion of this volume. That the Lord will use the book for spiritual refreshment and blessing is the chief desire of its compiler.

HELEN S. DYER.

ALDINGTON, KENT.

CHAPTER I

LINKS IN A CHAIN OF BLESSING

"*Ask of Me and I shall give thee the heathen for thine inheritance.*"

PENS more graphic than that of the present writer have endeavoured to depict in ways that should arrest attention, and compel thought, the vastness of the need of unevangelised countries; the fewness of the workers, and the immensity of the field.

The last three decades of the nineteenth century have seen a rapid development of missionary enterprise in India. Thirty years ago a large part of Central India was entirely without evangelistic effort. Mission stations were few and far apart. There was mission work in Bombay, Nagpur, Jabalpur and Allahabad, a leap of some hundreds of miles from station to station, and between—darkness. The beautiful valley of the Nerbudda, and the equally fertile province of Berar, with the Satpura hills between, had no missionary. Each of these contains numerous cities with swarming populations, and myriads of villages. It is marvellous to see how God has worked in covering these spiritually destitute tracts of country with spirit-filled workers.

In the early seventies God sent William Taylor (of Californian fame) to India. In the space of from two to three years he was used to convert scores of the English-speaking population in the large cities. These converts formed themselves into Methodist churches in Bombay, Calcutta, Madras, Lucknow, and elsewhere, and from the ranks of these converted Europeans, Eurasians and Indians, many grand gospel workers have been furnished. They and their children form the backbone of many Christian communities in India to-day.

The vastness of the field, and the scarcity of labourers, impressed deeply the heart of William Taylor. He sent an urgent call to America for men to come out to India as self-supporting missionaries. The call was heard. A small band of rugged, but consecrated, Christians responded. Some arrived in time to participate in the closing scenes of William Taylor's campaign ; others came to help carry on the work after he had left the country. Some settled as pastors of the churches of English-speaking people alluded to, and endeavoured, with the aid of their flock, to open out Native Mission work. Others went out into the jungle straight to the heathen. Some of these stalwarts are still in the field, some have retired, others have passed over the line from work to reward. It is impossible to estimate too highly the courage and self-denying toil of these pioneer labourers. The planting of the Gospel in Western India owes much to their zeal.

From that date there has been a continual series of developments. In less than ten years a number of new missions had been planted, many of them small in their inception, at first feeble and seemingly insignificant, but they were planted in faith, took root, and spread, and covered large tracts of the country hitherto unclaimed for Christ. One lone Englishwoman with a concern to be useful to the women of India was the frail plant which has grown into the Friends' Foreign Mission in the Nerbudda Valley, with its occupation of the important towns of Hoshangabad, Sohagpur, Seoni Malwa and Itarsi, with its large orphanages and industrial enterprises, and encouraging village settlements. The Swedish Mission has located in other towns on the borders. But it is of Berar, and the marvellous planting of the Gospel on that virgin soil, with which our narrative has to do.

In the cool season a trip through Berar is most enjoyable. It is a small compact province joined to Hyderabad State on the west and south, and to the Central Provinces on the north and east. It formerly belonged to the

Nizam of Hyderabad, but was assigned to the British Government by negotiation. The country is particularly well cultivated, and it is a pretty sight to pass by the cotton fields ripe for picking; the women, in their picturesque red or blue *sarees*, working away, and piling the cotton into little snow-like heaps as they gather it from the bushes. At the same time the jowari harvest is going on. Jowari is a tall-growing corn, with a large bunchy head. It is cheaper than wheat, and more commonly used in the country where it grows. The fields of linseed, with their bright blue blossoms; the yellow mustard, also grown for its oil; and the frequent herds of cattle, all diversify the scene, and indicate comfort and prosperity. Such is Berar in non-famine days.

One of the most attractive stations in Berar is Ellichpur. It is well wooded with shade trees and clumps of bamboos, and is bounded on the north by a fine range of hills, the Satpuras. On one of these is situated Chikalda, a beautiful hot weather retreat, about twenty miles from Ellichpur. A prominent object on another hill brow is the fortress of Gawilgarh. One hundred years ago (in 1802) this was stormed by the British army. The Mussulmans who were defending it believed it to be impregnable, but finding the foe was breaking through their walls, they turned, killed their women and children, and themselves escaped by an underground passage down a narrow defile. For many years Ellichpur was a depot for British soldiers, but has for some years now been garrisoned only by a small force of Native infantry. It has an English church and cemetery, but very few resident English-speaking families.

It was in Ellichpur, nearly thirty years ago, that the seed of the movement was first planted that has now covered Berar with a network of mission stations. How much of this steady extension has been the result of earnest believing prayer may never be known, but we believe that hundreds of workers have been prayed into the mission field in direct answer to the command of the Saviour (Matt. ix. 38). Here and there we meet with a reminiscence, and catch a glimpse of hearts burdened with prayers, which have afterwards been most preciously answered. It was so in this case.

Colonel G. W. Oldham, a Christian officer in the Government Engineering Department, then resident in Bombay, but now spending an honoured old age in London, writes :—

"In 1874 I was stationed in India, and at Christmas I went up to Ellichpur, in the north of the province of Berar, to spend Christmas with my wife. On New Year's Day we were cast down in spirit, because there was no messenger of the Lord caring for the people there. We spent nearly the whole of the day in prayer, asking God to send someone to work in Ellichpur, which is thirty-two miles from the nearest railway station, and therefore quite out of the world.

"Ten days afterwards I was returning to Bombay, and when I got to the railway station at Amraoti, the first man I saw was Albert Norton, an American, who had come to India in connection with William Taylor's mission. I asked him what he did there, and he replied: 'I am thinking of starting work at Ellichpur.'

"'Praise God,' I said, 'I did not think my prayer was to be answered so soon.'"

Mr Norton began his mission work in a very humble way, trusting in God to lead him forward. The money that enabled him to start for Ellichpur was a remittance from Bulgaria of eighty-seven rupees from a friend who had heard of his call to India, and was partly subscribed by quite poor people. He resolved to live very humbly, and at first boarded in a native hut. As news of his work and the wonderfully open doors in a needy field reached his circle in America, others were drawn to join him, and one to become his wife, who has ever since been his faithful co-worker in all his labours for the Lord. In the course of time they had a family of six sons, and as Col. Oldham testifies, "they led a wonderful life in India. And just as wonderfully were they fed as Elijah by the ravens. Sometimes an official sent them food, sometimes a native gentleman sent a basket of vegetables. Sometimes a note came from England or America with money, but they never knew where the money was to come from. And as the result of this one man's faith, over one hundred workers for the Lord have subsequently gone out to India."

CHAPTER II

CALLED AND QUALIFIED FOR A MISSIONARY CAREER

"*That our daughters may be as corner stones, polished after the similitude of a palace.*"

AMONG the earliest to respond to Mr Norton's call for fellow-labourers was Miss Jennie Frow, afterwards Mrs M. B. Fuller, whose life forms the subject of this volume. She was born in Winchester, Adam's County, Ohio, December 16th, 1851, the third daughter of Mr and Mrs John Frow of that city. A brief story of her early days has been tenderly outlined by her surviving sister, Mrs Margaret Donaldson, of Tavarez, Florida, who writes:—

"Our Jennie, the baby of the household, for nine years had no clouds to darken a happy care-free childhood. But at that age, when most needed, the life of a tender Christian mother went out, and the home and hearts of father and children were left desolate. Life went on with the accumulating interests of the years, when Jennie's education, at the age of sixteen, fitted her for the office of teacher.

She performed her duties with scrupulous conscientiousness, and made for herself a reputation as an instructor and disciplinarian which secured for her situations of trust and responsibility. During this period Jennie had much to bear, but the trials of life finally brought her to God.

"At the age of nineteen she studied farther at the Normal School at Lebanon, Ohio, in preparation for what she then thought would be her life work. In these years, while dealing with the hearts and minds of the young under her care, the Lord by His Spirit was dealing with her soul, and she was brought into a deeper Christian experience where she could hear His voice calling her to Gospel service in the 'regions beyond.' The conflict that this implied in her mind was the secret with her sister Margaret, who rejoiced with her when victory came and she was enabled to say 'Yes,' to the Lord. From this time the whole plan of Jennie's life was changed, and the first step of preparation was her going to Oberlin, Ohio, to enter college for a literary course. This was in 1873.

"From infancy her eyes spoke the language of her heart, and the buoyancy of her spirits in childhood and early womanhood, as well as after great burdens came into her life, brought joy to all about her. Her keen sense of humour and kindly spirit embellished by God's grace made her a congenial companion. Her love of the beautiful and of good cheer were inherent qualities which grace only intensified; even when her soul went through deep waters the sunshine of her spirit would beautify the clouds.

"As a daughter she was loyal, as a sister unselfish and loving. Words fail me to tell what she was to me. While I'm glad to-day in her gladness, yet there are times when the world seems very empty without her. Her ministry of love will not fail me in life, and will go on to life eternal. The whole secret of her fruitful life came from her love of the truth, and the joy of the indwelling CHRIST. Her true, transparent soul would have nothing but the truth, and while one's pen could bring out much that would seem like eulogy, we know she would say 'Not unto us, not unto us, O Lord, but unto Thy name give glory.'

"After entering college the enemy made a great fight to defeat the purpose to which she was so clearly called. But God was faithful, the battle was His, not hers, and she was compassed about with songs of deliverance, and never after questioned God's leading. From this time forward she followed every step, however difficult or seemingly impossible, in simple childlike faith. The fruit of her consecration and trust touched many lives for blessing."

It was in the closing years of the life of that great and good man, who made Oberlin famous as an evangelical centre, Charles G. Finney, that Jennie Frow joined the college as a student. In a letter to her sister Margaret, written at that time, she mentions her first glimpse of Mr Finney, and of the promised pleasure of an interview. The same letter gives bright and chatty details of her life in college, but breaks off in the middle with the remark: "I do not think of anything particular for the future now, only His glory. If it is His will for me to take a college course here He will open the way. If not I am

> 'Content to fill a little space
> If Thou be glorified.'"

Although the future was then hid from her eyes, the spirit of entire consecration to God's service, which led her out into the mission field, was already at work in her heart. The Lord was teaching her many things, and she was anxious to lead her much loved sister out into the fuller experiences of consecration and sanctification which she was pressing into herself. An indication this of one of the most necessary qualifications for service. Miss Jennie obeyed the command: "Go home to thy friends and tell them how great things the LORD hath done for thee" (Mark v. 19).

The enemy of souls tempted her for this, and warned her against writing home so much of her experience lest she should not "hold out."

But she based her experience on the Word of God—another life-long characteristic and sound qualification for the mission field. "These temptations," she says, "caused me to tremble at first, but now I know much that Jesus is able to do:—

Able to succour them that are tempted.—Heb. ii. 18.
Able to make me stand.—Rom. xiv. 4.
Able to do more than I can ask or think.—Eph. iii. 20.
Able to keep all I have committed to Him.—2 Tim. i. 12.
Able to build me up.—Acts xx. 32.
Able to keep me from falling.—Jude i. 24.
Able to subdue all things unto Himself.—Phil. iii. 21.

All this! and then Jesus asks, 'Believe ye that I am able to do this?' How can the answer be other than, 'Yea, Lord!'"

She then goes on to explain to her sister the beautiful simplicity of the way of holiness as follows:—

"I do realise that Jesus saves me just now. . . . To enter this way the first step is an entire consecration to the Lord. Laying ourselves on the altar, our reputation (willing to be called fools for Christ's sake), our time, talent, influence, tongue, loved ones, will, everything must be laid on the altar. That is all the part we have in the work. Consecration immediately precedes sanctification, and ever after accompanies it. Faith is the only condition of sanctification. Faith to believe God has promised it in His word; faith that He is able to perform; faith that He is willing, and that He does do it just now.

"Oh, it is nothing but believing that the past has had one glorious atonement made upon the Cross, so complete, and I had nothing to do with it—all done by the Son of God, and believing that the shed blood does cleanse from sin; believing also that God has taken your will as you laid it on the altar, you have nothing but His will, you leave the future in His hands, looking to Him moment by moment, believing that He does save you, for He is able to save to the uttermost.

"Satan will tempt you; but, Maggie dear, don't stop to argue with him, but flee right to Christ, saying, 'He is able to succour.' You can usually defeat Satan with a passage of Scripture, but if not enough, say 'Glory to the Lamb!' for the devil cannot bear to hear His name. Satan is making grand struggles for my soul, but Jesus saves me just now."

In the light of her after life and service for the Lord, it is beautiful to trace how wonderfully He was leading and qualifying this dear child of His for future usefulness in the mission field. Satan always makes strong fight for souls whom the Lord destines to use greatly in His service, but the measure of the fight is the measure of the victory, and leads up to the point of being able to help others that are tempted.

This same leading is manifest also in another aspect in her early life. The following she says did much to teach her how to trust the Lord for greater things :--

"I had been a Christian less than three years, when one summer, with a journey before me, I was resting in a village in Ohio. The seven dollars necessary for my railway fare I put on one side in my purse, and in one way and another I spent all the money I had remaining. As I was retiring for the night, with my trunk packed, and expecting the omnibus to call for me in the forenoon, the thought occurred to me that I had better count that money and see if it were all right. I did so, and, to my dismay, found it some cents short. I racked my memory in vain to remember where I had spent it, or what had become of it. I felt I could not tell any one of my difficulty, and how was I to leave in the morning with not enough money to pay my fare? Then, like many Christians, I began to worry. After a long time I fell asleep, and on awaking in the morning my difficulty like a cloud came upon me. It occurred to me to tell God all about it, and in so doing I had peace and quietness. In about half an hour I heard a rap at my door, and on opening it, found a gentleman there who handed me the exact sum, twenty-three cents. I asked him why he did it. He replied that one day in an emergency he had borrowed it of me, and had forgotten all about it until a little while ago. I had forgotten it, too, but God had not, and when I cried unto Him He delivered me by reminding this brother of that sum. But my story is not yet finished. In departing a friend, who was in poor circumstances, gave me a dollar. I refused to take it, feeling hers was the greater need, assuring her that I had enough. But she urged it upon me saying: 'You may need it to get something on the way.' I took it reluctantly to please her, secretly resolving in some way to return it. When I reached the city I found to my astonishment the fare was eight dollars instead of seven. Had not this dear woman given me the dollar I would have been alone in a great city without enough money for the rest of my journey. How God's care humbled me! He not only gave me the few cents I thought I needed, but supplied a need which He alone foresaw, and of which I was ignorant. It made a great impression on my mind. How true it is that He 'is able to do exceeding abundantly above all that we ask or think!'"

Incidents such as this, which she loved to

relate as evidences of God's care for His children, encouraged Miss Frow to step out in faith when the call came for wider service, and it was revealed to her that her life was to be given to God for India.

In the autumn of 1876 she was a member of the Literary graduating class at Oberlin, and was regarded as its best linguist. Her intention had been to graduate and then devote some time to teaching, until she should at least pay the expense of her College course. But at this juncture she was brought to face the question whether it was the Lord's will for her to leave her College course incomplete, and go at once to India as a missionary.

Her reply was characteristic and prompt. "I will pray about it. And I will ask God if He wants me to go to India at this time, that He will send money to pay what I am under an obligation to refund for my education, and enough also for my outfit and passage to India; but that if He does not want me to go now, that He will withhold the money."

In a few weeks the Lord had sent her the money, her own plans were broken off, and her way made perfectly clear to go to India. A part of the sacrifice no one knew but God. But He knew and accepted her all as she laid it on the altar, but afterwards returned the blessing to her life in overflowing measure.

In the beautiful story she tells of her praying

Irish friend, "Mary Ann," she relates that when she received her marching orders for India she was perplexed about leaving her sister Margaret, who was much of an invalid. Then in answer to prayer the Lord reminded her of Mary Ann. "I can never forget when asked if she would take my place and let me go. We could give her no remuneration, only a home, and the fact that she freed me to go. She received it as the call of God."

Her sister Margaret writes recalling this period: "When the time came in 1876 that the Lord said 'go forward,' the cords of love that bound Jennie to the hearts of her family were drawn taut. Our aged father held closely to his youngest born, but the Lord in His tender mercy spared him the pain of the separation by taking him to the heavenly mansions just three weeks before she was to sail for India. A dear brother and sister only were left of the ties of the flesh to surrender. Counting all things as nothing to follow the excellency of God's will for her, the pain of the good-bye lost its sting. To the sister came such a vision of the honour the Lord conferred upon her by calling her darling to such a glorious service, that when the farewell came the tears were stayed, and her heart said, 'Nay, Lord, I will not give Thee a weeping sacrifice.' In all the long years that followed, when the great waters rolled between us there was never any desire to take the offering from the altar."

Had Miss Frow applied, she could no doubt have been sent to India under the auspices of one of the large and established Missionary Boards. But her sympathies had been drawn out towards the pioneer faith work of Albert and Mary Norton at Ellichpur, and she felt that the Lord was calling her to that place as her future sphere of labour. She went out with no pledge of support from any human source, because she felt that thus her life would tell more for Christ and His Kingdom. One who knew her well at this time says that the influence of Mr Finney may be traced in this decision. He felt deeply that missionaries and preachers generally were handicapped and without power from on high, because they did not have faith to the extent of their duty and privilege. Duncan Matheson said: "Reality is the great thing; I have always sought reality." This was very true of our sister. It was an axiomatic truth with her that anything she might say would be of no weight unless backed by her life.

CHAPTER III

STEPS IN FAITH AND ANSWERS TO PRAYER

"*Take this child, . . . nurse it for Me, and I will give thee thy wages.*"

MISS FROW arrived in India on January 4th, 1877. "The motto of her missionary life from the beginning was, 'Have faith in God.' She seemed such a lonely little soul, but God was with her." So writes a life-long friend who met her for the first time when she landed, a stranger in a strange land, on the shores of India. Thus early indeed was Miss Frow's name added to that roll of honour, which, beginning in the eleventh of Hebrews, still goes on receiving additions wherever God's people step out in faith on His promises, in answer to His call. Like Abraham, Miss Frow went forth not knowing whither she went. She landed in Bombay without friends or promise of financial support; without special training for the mission field or knowledge of the country and people.

One seal of her call to India came to her on the voyage. Among her fellow-passengers was a pilot of Rangoon harbour, an English sea captain. He had been a hater of missions and missionaries. But the gentleness and Christlike character of our sister, who shone for Jesus amid the discomforts of an ocean voyage, touched his heart, and converted him to a friend of missions. He afterwards corresponded with her and sent money for her work.

Miss Frow received a warm welcome from Mr and Mrs Norton. Mr Norton came to Bombay to meet her and pilot her up to the wilds of Berar. Her early missionary experiences were not smooth, but they fitted her to endure hardness as a good soldier of Jesus Christ. She needed the full assurance of her call to India to enable her to hold on, and she had it. Later on she was wont to remark that the first two years in the field are always the most trying and difficult, and generally decide a young missionary's career.

Miss Frow served an apprenticeship of three and a half years at Ellichpur, part of the time with Mr and Mrs Norton, and part with Mr and Mrs Sibley, who took up the work there and enabled Mr Norton to branch out into labour among the Kurkus, the hill tribe inhabiting the southern slopes of the Satpura hills.

The records that remain of those days are meagre. Miss Frow gained a colloquial knowledge of Hindustani and Marathi, and learned to know and love the people. The usual duties of preaching and visiting were carried on side by side with the study of the language.

There was a severe famine in South India in 1877-8. It was some two to three hundred miles away from Berar, but Miss Frow's heart was stirred on hearing of missionaries in the affected district taking some of the orphans to train for the Lord. She felt she would like to have a share in such a blessed work. Mr Sibley was going to Bombay, and he was commissioned to meet Mr C. B. Ward of Bellary,[1] and receive from him six orphan girls and bring them back with him to Ellichpur. Mr Ward was gathering in large numbers of orphans in the Hyderabad country south of Sholapur. He was willing to give the girls but it was with some difficulty they were persuaded to go, and were taken back the long journey by road and rail to Ellichpur.

Most of them were mere skeletons, and it required the greatest care and watchfulness to save the lives of two or three of them. They were like little Arabs for wildness, with no conception of truth or honesty. In fact they were so depraved that the first efforts to train them seemed most discouraging. Finally, after six months, the most trying one, and the

[1] Now of Yellandu and Bastor. Mr Ward was one of William Taylor's stalwarts alluded to in Chapter I.

ringleader in mischief, came to Miss Frow and expressed sorrow for her bad conduct. The Spirit of God worked on their hearts and brought them wonderfully to see that they were sinners, and they all yielded themselves to Jesus for salvation.

A few weeks later Miss Frow received a letter from a Christian blacksmith in Ohio, telling her that at a certain time he had spent a whole evening in prayer to God for the conversion of these children, and for a spiritual uplift for her own soul. Miss Frow referred to her diary, and found that it was the very day that the first signs of penitence showed themselves in the children. He told her to take heart, for God had given him the assurance that all would be saved. Truly the uplift had come, and the incident was to Miss Frow ever after a goodly illustration of the text, "While they are yet speaking I will hear."

She had much cause to praise God for the change wrought in the children. They became truthful, asked for what they wanted instead of stealing it, and began to be industrious and obedient.

But there was one thing they did not seem able to comprehend, and that was how to pray. One little girl would kneel down and say over and over, "Lord, make me a good girl; Lord, make me a good girl." Then she would say "Amen," and think she had prayed.

In the mission house was a beautiful Persian cat which became the children's special pet. One evening pussy was missing, and the children were inconsolable; they thought it would be killed by a hyena or a jackal. When they gathered for evening prayer, Miss Frow proposed they should tell Jesus about the lost pussy, and ask that, if in accord with His will, it should be brought back safely. This was something real and definite to their minds, and they listened with a sort of awe.

Early in the morning a man appeared in the compound with something white under his arm. The girls saw it, and a shout went up, "Oh, Mamma, God has heard prayer; pussy has come back."

Miss Frow rejoiced that God had used this simple incident to teach them how to pray. And especially that the thought that their pet's return was an answer to prayer was uppermost in their minds. From that time they began to pray from their hearts. They realised that God was a Person who heard and knew and answered them, and it revealed to them His love and willingness in giving them back what was a great joy to them.

On a later occasion, when supplies ran short for their support, all were gathered for prayer. The eldest girl knelt and said: "O Lord, the young lions do lack and suffer hunger, but they that seek Thee shall never lack." And then followed with a simple petition that God would supply their need, and He did.

A beggars' service was held on the verandah of the Ellichpur mission house every Sunday. This is a common institution in India. Beggars of all sorts abound. There are the maimed, halt, lame, blind, young and old. It is easy to make known to this community that they are welcome at the mission house at a certain hour each Sunday and at no other time. And they come and listen to the Gospel message week in and week out, year after year, for the sake, in most cases, of the cup of rice, or other grain, or the small coin of money that is distributed to each at the close.

Among those who attended this service at Ellichpur was a blind boy, almost grown to manhood, whose eager clutch at the reward did not give much encouragement to hope that the truth was entering his heart. He would, however, frequently stand and listen to the preaching in the bazaar, and one Sunday presented himself, saying he desired to become a Christian. The missionaries were surprised that he had retained a knowledge of divine things, and told him to come again in the afternoon. He was there promptly, and told them he had been to his relatives to tell them he was going to become a Christian, and they asked him if he was going to become a

Christian for his stomach's sake. He said, "I told them 'Yes, for my stomach's sake,' for what could they understand?" Immediately, without any reproof from those present, he fell down on his knees, and cried out, "O Lord, save me from lying, and from all sin." He gave further evidence that his heart was genuinely touched, was baptised by the name of Bartimeus, and became a useful worker.

A small bungalow was secured at Chikalda, the little sanatorium on the hills, and formed a welcome hot weather resort when the heat in Ellichpur became too great. Going to Chikalda did not mean any cessation of labour for Miss Frow and her co-workers, they found their work wherever they went, and testified of the saving power of Jesus to the people at Chikalda as they did at Ellichpur.

A scrap of Chikalda experience may come in here, but as it has no date I do not know exactly when to locate it. Miss Frow wrote: "We have been very low in funds. Our box from home of fruits, etc., has been such a luxury and supplied all the lack of food we could not buy. We have had some royal meals out of that bean bag and the corn bag. Neither are exhausted yet. The night the money came which delivered us, one of the girls said to me, 'Mother, we will eat less.' My heart was so touched, but that night's mail brought twenty-four dollars from home. It is just wonderful how the dear Lord cares for us. We are so far from all provisions up here—eighteen miles—that even at the best our food has not much variety. We have had splendid success making tarts with the dried fruit after your recipe. To-day some officer who has been out hunting has sent us in a small leg of venison, and a jungle fowl.

"Thus the dear Lord does set a table in the wilderness. Oh why will men not put their trust in Him? 'The young lions do lack and suffer hunger, but they that seek the Lord shall not want any good thing.' But strange to say, my greatest faith text for daily bread is this: 'Seek ye first the Kingdom of God and His righteousness, and all these things shall be added unto you.'"

CHAPTER IV

MISS FROW BECOMES MRS FULLER

"*I being in the way the Lord led me.*"

A SEVERE attack of jungle fever, followed by a relapse of the same, made it imperative for Miss Frow to seek a lengthened rest, and led to her return to America in August, 1880.

At this time an acquaintance was renewed which had been laid upon the altar on her call and departure to India, with the result that Miss Frow was united in marriage to Marcus B. Fuller, an old friend and fellow student, who was now prepared to devote his life also to the service of God in India. The marriage took place at her sister's home at Lodi, Ohio, on April 6th, 1881. Early in 1882 Mr and Mrs Fuller left America for England on their way to India.

Mrs Fuller was unable during this furlough to do so much as she desired in arousing interest in India's needs, but in a quiet way was made a blessing to many. In all her furloughs home (says her sister) there was an eagerness to return to the land of her adoption, and to her work there as a precious trust, put into her hands, as she felt, by the King of Heaven.

It may seem incredible to some readers, and to others intensely imprudent, for these young people to start on their way to India without sufficient means to complete the journey. They met with opposition and discouragement from home friends in taking this course, but they saw before them the Lord guiding and leading, and were content to follow. Among the few letters which have been preserved, some relate to this journey, and we find that Mrs Fuller thoroughly enjoyed the experience. She again proved the Lord's care and gracious providing Hand, and praised Him for so ordering their journey as to permit them to enjoy several weeks in London and a visit to Scotland also. Some passages from these letters will help the story.

London, *March 9th*, 1882.—"We spent two weeks at Dr Boardman's, and then took a room near by. We get our own breakfasts, and are usually out for dinner and tea. Mark and I enjoy being alone, a luxury we have not had much since we have been married. I have learned to love the Boardmans very much. They have a meeting for holiness every Tuesday. I do not think I ever attended a meeting so profitable and so full of instruction. Since Dr Boardman has published his book on healing by the prayer of faith, so many have written to him, and God uses him wonderfully in this line of work. . . . Truly, as of old, 'I am the Lord that healeth thee.' I understand this faith as never before. . . . Oh, I realise, as in all spiritual things, it is easy to get hold of it theoretically, and not practise it. I was taught a simple lesson by an old woman when we were in Scotland. Mark had been preaching, and when he came down from the pulpit he saw this dear old woman with a bright face, and he asked her if she were a Christian. 'Oh yes,' she replied boldly. And her boldness led Mark to suppose she had been one some time. So he continued: 'How long have you been a Christian?' 'Oh, just since you have been preaching.' Wonderful decision of soul. She saw the truth and grasped it at once. How much we lose by not making a promise our own the moment the Spirit illuminates it to us. Oh, let us live up to the light we receive, and make instant decision of soul as soon as we see the truth. I saw I was to give my body to Christ as His body. 'Therefore glorify God in your body, and in your spirit, *which are God's.*'

"Our visit here has been such a blessing to us. So many things have been made clear to me. How kind the dear Lord has been. There has one difficulty assailed me in my spiritual life, and it is only this last year that I have been coming out of it. It was throwing away my confidence. When I first became a Christian, I would sin or my feelings would go, and then the devil would whisper, 'You can't be a Christian and feel this way, or do this way. You are deceived.' I would listen and say, 'That's so,' and throw away my confidence, and for days and weeks be in darkness and unhappy. Then I would have to come back to the Lord and do the first works over again. I did that many times, till I learned Satan's device. Then, when the devil would say, 'See here, you can't be a Christian,' instead of throwing away all God had done for me, I would reply, 'Well, if I am not a Christian, it is high time I became one. I will get down on my knees and become one.' That broke the power of the devil there. Well, I ceased to have any doubts as to my acceptance, when the same snare would be spread for me later on.

"I sought again and again for the baptism of the Holy Spirit, and God gave it to me. Then I would ask Him to make me more like Himself. To do this He would have to show me what hindered, and the sight of some bit of self in my heart would throw me into despair. I would say, 'Could such a heart as that have the baptism of the Holy Ghost?' and away would go my confidence. Well, darkness would be the result, until I came back to Him. Perhaps it was some precious testimony or experience which was different from mine, and I would say, 'I have nothing like that,' and away would go my confidence. Or perhaps it was the experience of some one far ahead of me, and in perfect despair I would say, 'I can never attain to that,' and away would go my confidence again. Over and over I have done this, but now I have learned to hold fast my confidence. If the Lord shows me some bit of self in my heart, I have learned to thank Him. How He must love us to take such pains to let nothing remain that hinders our very prayer to be like Him. If some one is far ahead of me, He helps me not to go into despair, but to thank Him for the new light. He will bring us through in His own way. 'Cast not away therefore your confidence, which has great recompense of reward.' I need patience to let the Lord mould me as He will, not dictating to Him how to do it. I have given up all hope of self to expect anything from self, but to have all things in Christ. 'Let us come boldly.' I have lost so much by feeling I would not have this or that, I was so unworthy. That is not true humility. The Lord likes to have us bold.

"Once in India when some disapproved of me, and I felt so downcast that maybe God did too, I asked Him to give me just one verse to show how He viewed me. Trembling for fear it would be some condemnation, I went to the Bible and got these words: 'He that toucheth you toucheth the apple of His eye.' I drew back; I thought I must be mistaken. I could not think that I was the apple of His eye. So I pled that He would speak to me once more. Again were the same words given me. But I could not believe it. I said, 'Dear Lord, don't be grieved with me. Try me just once more, and I will not ask again.' Again the third time I got the same words. Oh, do let us take God at His word. It is true we are unworthy, but He never expects us to be worthy. We never can be, but it grieves Him when we do not take Him at His word. He does these things for us for His own sake.

"The Spirit once revealed to me, as I was feeling my prayers did not avail, that I was secretly trying to recommend myself to God; that on account of my goodness or faithfulness He would hear me. I started back. Oh! I came only in Jesus' name. The first petition we learned at our mother's knee, 'for Jesus' sake,' sometimes takes years for us to know what it means. There can never be any good thing in me. I have *all* things in Christ. 'All things are yours . . . and ye are Christ's.' And I can only do through Him. May the Lord find us thus empty that He can work through us. . . .

"We have learned so much in our visiting

time here. How precious it has been. Dear Mark has always wanted to spend a few weeks in England. If we had had the money to go on direct to India we would have been on our way. But God had better things in store for us, and we have been detained. He keeps adding to our store of passage money. I was asked to speak at the Y.M.C.A. Rooms. When I got through, a dear man, a Christian publisher, put a sovereign in my hand. Last evening I went out with Mrs B. The gentleman of the house had said nothing to me, but on hearing I was a missionary asked me what Board I was under. I told him that we had no pledged support. Without a word—God inclined his heart—he laid twenty shillings in my hand. We went from there to a drawing-room meeting. God helped me to speak, but not concerning missions. We had only spent a few pence for omnibus hire to get there, but the friends made us take five shillings for expenses. Mrs Boardman insisted on my having the balance.

"I came home and found Mark, and laid it little by little in the palm of his hand. He retaliated by showing a letter which had contained five pounds. The writer said it had been sent her for a certain purpose which had already been provided for, and so she had great joy in sending it on to me.

"Thus God gives us our hire, and when He

lifts the pillar of cloud and fire with the command 'Go forward,' we shall have enough and to spare. When the fragments are measured sometimes there are twelve baskets over.

"Mark said the other day at breakfast: 'We could not have felt that it was best for us to stay so long, nor would our friends have thought it a wise use of money, but God managed it.' How truly they that trust in Him are never confounded!

"I want you to pray much for us and feel it your work as much as if you were in the field. I have had wondrous views of what God wants to do at Ellichpur. You and Mary Ann can help us as if you were with us. Feel it your work as well as ours."

London, March 20th.—"Dearest ones, we are off for Bombay this week. We sail Wednesday. The Lord has been indeed good to us in letting us stay so long in London. It has been so rich in blessing to our souls. You will hear from us several times on our way to Bombay. Hurrah! I feel like a bird. I can hardly wait to get there. 'Thou openest Thine hand and satisfiest the desire of every living thing.' Have not we proved it true! We learn that Brother Sibley is expecting to come to Bombay to meet us. Is not that splendid!"

Nearing Port Said, s.s. Ancona, April 3rd, 1882.—"You will see by our letter to N——

that up to within one day of Malta we had very rough weather from Gibraltar. That last day we felt was given us in answer to prayer. 'He knoweth our frame.' We found ourselves in Malta bright and early on Thursday morning. The only young lady on board had had her trunks left behind, and I agreed to go ashore with her to procure clothing. It adds to the interest of the place to know the Apostle Paul was once here. On landing we were besieged by men wanting to act as guides. One man with a carriage followed us a long way. He seemed to feel that we would lose our way and be forced to take him. But he did not know that we had the God of Jacob with us. I lifted up my heart that we might find some English person to speak to. Then we sat to rest, for we were all tired out with our climbing up the steep narrow street. As we sat an English lady, dressed in black, hurriedly passed us. I eagerly touched her arm and she kindly directed us to the main thoroughfare, to an English shop where we could get what we wanted and the prices were fixed. Once in the cool shop with a bona-fide English girl to wait upon us, filled us with gratitude.

"I cannot tell you how I enjoyed those hours on land. The air so fragrant and balmy! Such flowers, beautiful roses, geraniums, heliotrope, pansies, etc., and orange trees bearing both blossoms and fruit. But one o'clock was the hour set for sailing, and we must get back to the ship, so leaving all the beauty (which, like everything else, has its alloy in beggars, etc.), we stepped into a little boat and were rowed back with our hands full of packages, rough baskets of oranges and lemons and our flowers. And how tenderly we have been shielded since. The sea has been so smooth and there has been no rocking until last evening and to-day. To-morrow morning early we anchor at Port Said."

April 4th.—"We entered the Canal this forenoon. . . . We are both so well. Sometimes I am a wonder to myself. When I think how I realised all this dimly *by faith* when we began to get ready, I can see it was God leading us, else we would never have had the courage to go through all the opposition and discouragement we received. It is nearly three months since we left you, and I never spent such a blessed three months in my life. We have learned so much; it has been full of teaching. Oh, if I could sit down by you and recount it all step by step it would fill your heart full of praise too. Unbelief has been the cause of all my spiritual troubles, and of many temporal ones also. 'He is faithful that promised.'"

Chikalda, May 2nd, 1882.—"When we reached Aden and I realised we were less than a week's journey from India, it seemed too good to be true. The last two nights on ship-board I could not sleep well. My heart was pressed so full. We landed on Tuesday, April 18th, and Mark and I arose very early that we might catch the first glimpse of land —*the* land of our adoption. Soon we discerned it like a shadow upon the water. Bolder and bolder it became until I could distinguish the familiar parts of the harbour, and soon the city itself lay stretched out before us—Bombay. Yes, India. I could only offer my life afresh to Him to use according to His own purpose and glory in this dark land.

"How eagerly I watched the boats coming off to the ship, to catch the glimpse of a familiar face. Friends met friends; but none came for us, and I turned downstairs to my cabin. Soon I heard my name, and there stood Mr Mody, a converted Parsee, and now a missionary in Bombay. To his greeting he added the words, 'Mr Sibley is on deck with your husband.' Soon we had each other by the hand, and oh what memories of days spent in work together at dear old Ellichpur crowded in upon me. We were like three little children. The tears were very near the surface, and when we arrived at the home of Mr Mody how sweet it was to fall upon our knees in praise and thanksgiving. We stayed two days in Bombay getting our baggage off and other business attended to, and on Thursday morning turned our faces Ellichpur-ward. The heat in Bombay was great though tempered by a delicious sea-breeze, but we knew our journey up country would not be thus tempered. And yet how God did shield us. It was a wonderful journey, which we will all ever remember. We were from 8 A.M. Thursday till 7.30 A.M. Friday reaching our railway station. We stayed until evening in the travellers' bungalow before venturing to start for Ellichpur.

"Dear, faithful Abraham met us at the station. At last we were on our way. The journey grew shorter and shorter. Our hearts were full. We had had nothing but mercies all the way. Our God had encompassed us about. As our wheels crushed the gravel walk up to the door, first Mrs Sibley came out, then all the girls and native Christians, although it was only 2 A.M. In the morning we had a thanksgiving service.

"I cannot tell you my emotions as I looked into the faces of the dear native Christians and remembered so vividly the days when we toiled on alone, when the heavens seemed brass, when we were as a sparrow on the housetop, and now how God had enriched us! As I went about and saw the answered prayers, how full of praise I became! There was one thing I had asked of God more than two years ago. I had had no intimation that it had ever been answered, and yet here it was so richly answered. How it taught me to wait upon God. Then I wish you could have *felt* the contrasts in the girls as I did. The wild untutored children who came to us, and the womanly girls with us now, it would do your heart good.

"We are prone to call ourselves 'a little mission,' and yet my deep conviction in coming back after a twenty months' absence is this, which I have said over and over to myself: 'THIS IS A VINE OF HIS OWN PLANTING.' Pray much for the labourers and waterers.

"We came up to Chikalda in a few days as the heat in Ellichpur was very great. The Sabbath before we left we had a communion service. Mark preached in English and Mr Sibley addressed the native Christians in Hindustani. This remembrance of His death was never before so precious. It was a blessed season to us all. What shall we render to the Lord for all His benefits? We could do nothing but give back our lives to Him to be used as He wished.

"We had quite an experience getting up to Chikalda, and Mark got his first taste of the vicissitudes of Indian travel. I came in a palanquin, the others by the new road in the coach with the children in a cart. Both had bad bullocks, and the time they had with them!

They expected to meet me here in the morning, but were detained over until another night at the halfway place. They had the keys and the money. Everything was locked, but I borrowed some food and got along nicely. Our experiences in getting settled would make you smile. Our water supply is a mile away, and the leathern bag in which it is brought burst, so that for a few days we were limited to a very little water, and that had a bad taste. We all took colds. The mat-man who had agreed to cover our floors failed to put in an appearance, but we finally got settled, and our rooms, furnished with the gifts of you dear ones, are a little home-like. . . .

"My days are full and busy. How I wish you could see the girls, and how hard they try to please. Shanti (Peace), the oldest girl, is growing into such a beautiful Christian, and is such a solid comfort and help to me, so steady and trustworthy. She knows she is dull, and how she seeks God's help to learn, and how He gives it! If you had been in the native prayer meeting this afternoon, you would have been touched by her testimony, as we all were. Six heathen were present, and listened attentively.

"Shanti said: 'Before I was a Christian, I sinned without a care. I lied, stole, quarrelled, etc., without any concern. I cannot do so now. If I sin, I am so sad, and when I am victor over sin it is such joy.' That is a meagre translation of her words, but she told me afterwards of her struggle with God's Spirit. 'He would tell me to speak; then I would question, Would it be proper to say this before all? But the Spirit would say in my heart, Speak, speak! And finally it came that in refusing I would only incur more sin, and I begged His help and power, and spoke.'

"I do so enjoy the Bible lesson with the girls. We have the Life of Christ under consideration, and it would do you good to see them with their Bibles. We have eight girls now with the baby. I do not know how long we will be able to keep Tara, the new girl, but she is 'a bud of promise,' and I hope she has been given us for her good. I wish you could see their sewing, it is really very nice. They have so much to tell me, so the sewing class is a very chatty hour. They have improved so under Mrs Sibley's care."

CHAPTER V

BUSY YEARS IN AKOLA

"*Kept by the power of God through faith.*"

THE spiritual destitution of Berar as a whole pressed heavily upon the souls of the few workers at Ellichpur. Much prayer was made for this needy province, and before twelve months had passed it was made clear to Mr and Mrs Fuller that they should branch out and open work for God in one of the other large cities of Berar, where no flag for Christ yet floated on the breeze. The Akola district was chosen, and a few months passed at the town of Akote, but a final settlement was made at Akola, a town on the main line of railway, about one day's journey nearer to Bombay than Ellichpur. A graphic picture of their experiences at this time comes from Mrs Fuller's own pen:

"We were detained for a few months on our way to our new station by a flooded river, so we took rooms in a large Government building in which were several families. Our next door neighbour was the owner of three large powerful dogs. One of them had been bitten by a mad dog, but, loth to part with it, he refused to kill it, and as time passed, it had been almost forgotten.

"One Saturday night, while my husband was suffering from fever, one of these dogs, called 'Fanny,' came in our back porch and kept leaping over the chairs and table. It kept us awake. I hunted the house over for a large riding whip to give her a blow or two, and thus, as I thought, teach her never to come again. But I could not find it. It was God's hidden care of me, and I knew it not. So I opened the door and bade her go. Had I struck her she might have leaped upon me. How God covered me in the time of danger I came afterwards to know.

"The next day, as we were preparing for our weekly service, I heard my husband cry out, 'Shut the door at once, and call in the servants. Fanny is mad, and has the M.'s servant pinned down to the ground.' It seemed hours, though only a few moments elapsed, before a gun was fired; the dog was dead, and the poor man freed with an ugly bite in his arm. We did all we could for him, but he died from hydrophobia nearly two months afterwards. It was a great shock to me, though deeply touched with God's protecting care. Truly He had covered us with His feathers.

"Not long afterwards we moved on to our new station. The town was over-run with half starved mangy dogs that no one owned or cared for. They invaded our premises and stole our fowls and everything they could get at. My husband shot one or two that were very troublesome, and one that was really mad. Now an orthodox Hindu will not take the life of anything, not even of an insect. In their belief in the transmigration of souls, they fear some deceased relative or friend might be in the animal or insect, and it would be murder. Pious Hindus take the greatest precautions. A fine young man once, assuming to be an enquirer, came to me to be taught the Bible. He adroitly turned the conversation to the Ten Commandments. When we reached 'Thou shalt not kill,' he attacked me hotly with accusations of taking life. It was evidently the sole object of his visit.

"Now this place we were living in was very bigoted, and the fact that my husband shot three dogs caused much talk. The devil took advantage of it to break up almost every open-air service. One evening my husband came home heart-sick and weary, saying, 'Oh! if God would deliver us from this dog question!' We knelt and committed the whole matter in prayer to Him. In a short time deliverance came through a most painful circumstance. We were sent for to visit a man who was ill.

My husband went and found it was hydrophobia, and it proved fatal.

"After all was over I went to the house with a word of sympathy. He was a fine young fellow of high caste and much beloved. His caste men gathered around me, and one old man said sadly, 'Madam, your husband is right, he is right,' and a murmur of approval ran through the crowd. The whole subject of my husband taking life was dropped from that day. And not only that, but if they suspected a dog was mad, they would beg him to come and shoot it."

In the years of their life at Akola, Mr and Mrs Fuller followed the same lines of faith in God for the supply of all their needs. One who knew them well at this time says: "Their life was not an easy one; but like Israel of old[1] they were tested and prepared to lead others in the way of faith. Making Akola their headquarters, they itinerated in the surrounding villages as well as preached the Gospel in the native city, worked among the educated natives, and testified to the Europeans in Berar.

"Mrs Fuller had the gift of sympathy with all classes of people. There was nothing priggish or exclusive about her religion. She took people as she found them, and met them in their special circumstances of need. Children

[1] Deut. viii. 3

were gathered in and cared for. Many workers came to join their mission, but one of the trials of this period was that few continued with them, and Mrs Fuller learned by experience the peculiar difficulties of union in faith mission work. Instead of being exempt from trial they seemed to pass through every kind of trial that they might learn how to succour others. As the years passed there did not seem to be as much progress or so great results as faith had led these devoted workers to expect. In waiting upon God in prayer, He sometimes gave wonderful visions of what He was going to do—and still the vision tarried. In the light of after years we can see how all these experiences and preparation were necessary to fit Mr and Mrs Fuller to be leaders of that large band of missionaries of the Alliance Mission which God was about to lead forth from America. They became thoroughly well versed in all branches of missionary work and missionary trial, and obtained a thorough knowledge of Marathi, to the careful study of which Mrs Fuller attached great importance."

During these years a little family was growing up around them. The best of Mrs Fuller's life was given to God and His service, but next to that came her children. How she loved them and watched over them and coveted every permissible pleasure and indulgence for them. Any kindness shown to her children always lived in her heart and called forth her warmest gratitude. But griefs as well as joys came with the children. Two sweet little girls, Margaret and Faith, buds of promise, were early taken to the heavenly home.

Besides the care of her little ones, a strenuous part was taken by Mrs Fuller herself in all the lines of work enumerated. When Mr Fuller was absent itinerating in the villages the burden of the Mission at Akola rested on her frail shoulders. She has told some pathetic stories of her life at this time. For her there was no regular relief and change as the hot season came round, such as is considered necessary for most Europeans who live on the burning plains of India. For six years she and her husband found it impossible to take a journey together. But there came a time when, after an illness, she was in a very low bodily condition, tormented with neuralgia and racked with pain and sleeplessness. She says: "I needed a change of air, and to go to the dentist's, but was too weak to take the journey alone to Bombay with three little children, so my husband accompanied us. I can never tell anyone the luxury of that journey—to have no care or responsibility; nothing to do but to let everything go into my husband's hands, and rest! If little Margaret fretted, or was hungry, he soothed her. If the older children were restless, he restrained them. When we changed trains late in the evening I did not have to think of the luggage. I did just what he told me to do, and he took all the responsibility. How delicious the sense of abandonment was! I can never foget it. Afterward a Voice said: 'If you would let all your life and work go into My Hands, I would take all the care and responsibility of everything, and you might rest and be free.' Yes, I understood it afresh. I could let go the strain and push and care, and let the government be upon His shoulder. I knew then what it meant by 'casting all your care upon Him, for He careth for you.'"

To the glory of God, and as an illustration of how real the promises and comforts of His love were made to her soul, she related the above and other incidents. At another time of prostration and weakness she was dreading the approach of the hot season, which is also the season of Hindu weddings—a season of brass bands, torchlight processions, and general noise and tumult, especially at night, to which their house in the native city was peculiarly exposed. She wrote: "As one procession passed our door my courage failed. The drumming seemed all on the top of my head, and I felt I could never endure days of it. Something said, 'You must get away from here,' and not realising that it was temptation,

I responded 'Yes,' while my brain was busy with plans of escape. Then these words came: 'No, do not go away. These are God's circumstances. He is able to deliver you. Underneath are the Everlasting Arms.' I did just what I should have done at first, I let go clinging to God, let go my fears and just dropped down into the Everlasting Arms. Oh, what rest! I did not have far to drop, and they felt so solid. . . . Not only did my heart get rest and peace from its fears and anxiety, in the willingness to let God care for my surroundings, but He did not let that procession pass the house again. It was no longer a theory—I knew how to drop into the Everlasting Arms."

The orphanage work begun at Ellichpur with the six famine orphans, as previously related, was continued and augmented at Akola. Boys as well as girls were received. Industrial works were established under the care of James P. Rogers, a skilled mechanic of American birth, but descended from the English martyr, "Master John Rogers" (as Foxe terms him), who suffered for his faith in the days of Queen Mary. These works were opened with the view of training the boys in habits of industry. They were thus among the pioneers of Industrial Mission work, a subject which the recent five years of famine has forced upon Indian Missions generally.

A product of the old plan of training boys in mission schools was thus described by another writer, after a trying experience of attempting to get several youths of the same class to engage in manual labour. "Yesu Das was sure he could preach, had never been converted, could not cook, never learned any sort of work, not strictly honest, either in tongue or fingers—but a candidate for the ministry of Jesus Christ; self-assured of his fitness for such work."

Mr and Mrs Fuller gave much thought to this question, and to the whole future of the Indian Christian Church with the view, so far as their share of the problem was concerned, of raising up a self-reliant, independent, self-propagating Christian community. Visitors to their workshop have been much struck with the element of cheerful briskness and sturdy independence that pervaded the place.

In 1883, Mr Fuller took into the orphanage a boy named Kunwadi, the son of a Madras cook, who had died in Akola. From the school he graduated into the workshop, where he became an expert carpenter, and after a time foreman. He continued his studies after leaving school, and applied his mind to mechanical engineering. Three years ago a public examination on this subject, open to the Bombay Presidency, was held in Bombay. Kunwadi went up for this, and out of a class of over thirty he passed second, only missing one question in three days' examination. Six high caste Brahmins, who had gone through a Government Training College in Akola, went up for the same examination. They were arrayed in fine silk garments, while Kunwadi went barefoot and plainly dressed. On meeting him, these Brahmins asked Kunwadi what *he* was there for, and laughing at him told him he would not pass, for what did he know, being a Christian? On the first day these six Brahmins made a complete failure, while the despised Christian went through successfully.

Kunwadi is not only a Christian in name, but an earnest evangelist in his spare hours; and at the time of writing is in sole charge of the workshops during Mr Rogers' absence on furlough.

It is the practice of the majority of missions in India to shape their school work to fit in with the Government Education Code, place the schools under Government inspection, and thus obtain a grant in aid per *capita* of children passed. The Akola Mission has always been an exception to this. Part of the Government revenue being raised by the opium and liquor traffics, Mr and Mrs Fuller from the first felt they could have no complicity with these evils by taking Government money. When asked why they refused a Government grant for their industrial training school, Mr Fuller replied:

"A dying Scotchman called his sons around him, and told them what he had to leave them, and how they should divide it among themselves. He then said: 'My sons, it is not much that I have accumulated for you, but remember this, there is not a dirty shilling among it!' There are too many 'dirty shillings' in the revenue of the Government of India for me to receive such money for God's work. I would not receive a donation for our work from a liquor or opium seller; and as long as Government continues to be the sole manufacturer and wholesale dealer in opium, I will not receive its money for our work. It is said that Government must have the revenue. When I visit the opium hells, the schools where men are graduated into perdition, I say to myself, 'If Government must destroy men, soul and body, for revenue, then *I will lessen the need a little by refusing the grant for our school.*" Mr and Mrs Fuller were not solitary in this practical form of protest against a giant wrong, but were in a very small minority. In mentioning it here, it is well to notice that though it was yet the day of small things, sound foundations were being laid for the future to build upon.

Along with the native children taken by Mrs Fuller into the orphanage were some of Eurasian or semi-European parentage. It was not possible to train the two classes together, so a separate department was opened for the latter. Miss Helen F. Dawlly came out from America to take charge of these children, and took them entirely out of Mrs Fuller's hands. Some time later the Anglo-Indian Orphanage was removed to Poona as being a more healthy place, with better educational advantages. Miss Dawlly died in 1893. Others have built on her foundation, and a large and successful work among a most neglected class is now being carried on, still on the same lines of faith in God for supplies by which it was commenced by Mrs Fuller and continued by Miss Dawlly.

Other helpers came but they had to get acclimatised and to learn the language, and still much of the burden of the work rested on Mrs Fuller. Once the care of the orphanage was left to her single-handed, through a hot season, in which she had been expecting to get a rest and change. Her co-worker, who should have relieved her at this time, had a most tempting offer of a sojourn in the hills. In the generosity of her soul Mrs Fuller said "Go." Though it cost her some conflict she felt that God would have her remain in Akola. Then Isa. xl. 29-31 was made very real to her. Like a glad song it fell upon her ears, "They shall run and not be weary, and they shall walk and not faint." She said: "These verses were translated into my life for that hot season. I arose in the strength they gave me, and went about my work contentedly, praying that at least a way might be prepared for my husband to have his rest, knowing he would not willingly leave me with all the added care. A most unexpected matter of business called him away for a week, and while gone a lovely offer was made him to remain with a friend we both loved, to study and assist in a work with the educated classes. With much difficulty he was persuaded to do this. The heat was very great. The orphanage was not properly finished; we had only one living room. I conducted four Marathi services a week, and had all the orphanage, with its endless petty cares to see to. I studied with my pandit one hour a day, and nursed a sick child for two or three weeks night and day.

"And yet I did not mind the heat. It often seemed as if a shadow rested on the house protecting me, and when it was all over, and they all came home, I could not see but that I was as rested and refreshed as they. If I had only learned then to abide in that strength, how much it might have saved me!"

In writing to her sister she mentions the difficulty of getting support for the uninteresting children in the orphanage, and says: "I have for some unexplainable reason rebelled inwardly from writing letters praising up a child to get money for its support. How many children at home do you know that you could write a letter about that would satisfy the public demand? I wish friends at home loved the Lord enough to be willing to send money labelled 'For the support of an orphan child to be trained for Christ.' . . . I am afraid I am sadly out of tune with the way work has often had to be done, that must be stimulated by something interesting instead of downright love to Christ." This love of truth and hatred of all shams was a very pronounced feature in Mrs Fuller's character, and showed itself in a variety of ways.

While the orphanage claimed so much of her time and thought, her spirit was by no means in bondage to her surroundings. She took the world and its needs into her horizon and brought all in prayer before the Throne. In the same letter she writes: "My heart has been much stirred of late, thinking over Afghanistan, Beloochistan, and the places of the earth still unopen to the Gospel. I wish I could go to them and lift up Christ. I believe the day is fast coming when God will do the work of a thousand years in one day. Praise His Name! We kept the day of prayer for missions, and it was a very sweet time to us. We were much blessed in lifting up our hearts for the dark places of the earth. The earth seems very little and God's heart of love very great, and the plan of redemption so ample.

Oh for the time when the knowledge of the Lord shall fill the earth."

Miss Carrie Bates (now Mrs Rogers), who joined Mrs Fuller in 1889, became one of her most faithful helpers. It was to Miss Bates' care that Mrs Fuller entrusted the orphanage and other work when in the autumn of 1890 she was able to leave India for a furlough to the home land. Mrs Rogers writes: "I have had an intimate acquaintance with Mrs Fuller since the beginning of 1889. We have worked together and shared our joys and sorrows. I shall never cease to thank God for what she has been to me. Her many deeds of kindness come often before me. Many times have we united in prayer for the work which always lay so near her heart.

"During the rains of 1890 the subject of enlargement was laid heavily upon our hearts, and Mrs Fuller proposed our meeting together every night for a week to unite in special prayer for more workers. There were only four of us at the time, and no human prospect of any others joining us. But the Lord was talking with us, and Mrs Fuller would quote verse after verse that He had given her: 'Enlarge the place of thy tent, and let them stretch forth the curtains of thine habitations: spare not, lengthen thy cords, and strengthen thy stakes; for thou shalt break forth on the right hand and on the left; and thy seed shall inherit the Gentiles, and make the desolate cities to be inhabited,' Isa. liv. 2, 3. 'Produce your cause, saith the Lord; bring forth your strong reasons; saith the King of Jacob,' Isa. xli. 21. 'Concerning the work of My hands command ye Me,' Isa. xlv. 11; and many other passages. That fall she went to America with her two children, her heart full of zeal and enthusiasm for the enlargement of the work. She passed through many testings and dark places, but never surrendered her faith, and God honoured her in it."

CHAPTER VI

A WIDENING SPHERE

"With my staff I passed over this Jordan, and now I am become two bands."

ALMOST every incident that Mrs Fuller's own pen has recorded, whether concerning her own life or that of others, has been of soul-dealing with God, answers to prayers, or lessons learned in the school of Christ. Of her visit to America in 1890-92, a visit fraught with important consequences to herself and others, as well as to her field of labour in India, she has left several such incidents on record.

I have stated that Mrs Fuller welcomed hard lessons that she might thereby be fitted to teach others. She said that "the only way to be able to sow the incorruptible seed of the Word in other hearts is to first have it made real to ourselves in some time of need." On this voyage to America some little time was spent visiting friends in Scotland. It was late autumn, and on inquiring for a passage to America, Mrs Fuller was told by the agent that the larger steamships were crowded at that season, and no berths obtainable. She was therefore induced to take passage on a line of which she knew nothing, although assured by the agent that it was good and safe. The friend she was visiting had misgivings about the ship chosen, but gave her as a parting message: "Let everything that hath breath praise the Lord." In a cloud of rain and mist Mrs Fuller and her little ones boarded the ship at Liverpool. She wrote: "A more cheerless scene I had not faced for many a day. The deck was wet and the steps were muddy. I knew no one. The second-class saloon was small and badly lighted, and the stewards were careless. I wanted to sit down and cry: but I did not. I saw no retreat out of it, and how I was to endure until I reached New York I did not know. Then there was the added bitterness that my friend was right, and that I had made a mistake.

"When we had passed Queenstown, the wind increased and the waves arose. How can I describe the days that followed! The storm grew in violence. We were ten days getting to the banks of Newfoundland. Ropes had to be stretched for the stewards and men to hold as they walked about. The officers said they had not encountered such a storm in ten years. I could not stand, and there was nothing to do but lie in my berth day after day. The food was poor, and I could not eat. Every few minutes a great wave would crash against the bow of the ship, break over the deck, and come down the companion-way, and slush up past my cabin door.

"How often the vision of my friend at the carriage window saying, 'Let everything that hath breath praise the Lord,' came up before me, and I was enabled to praise Him. But the Word that held me was: 'God is faithful, who will not suffer you to be tempted above that ye are able; but will with the temptation make also the way to escape, that ye may be able to endure it' (1 Cor. x. 13, R.V.). Over and over did it seem as if I could never endure it. And God would reply: 'Ye shall not be tempted above what ye are able to bear.' And somehow I came to *know* that I should not be. In every deep trial since, I know that it will not be above what I am able to bear, and that God will prepare a way to escape.

"When we reached the banks, and had outridden the storm, and had glided into smooth waters, how sweetly the words came to me: 'He maketh the storm a calm, so that the waves thereof are still. Then are they glad because they be quiet' (Psalm cvii. 29, 30). Four days more and we were anchored in New York.

"But so deep was the submission that God wrought in my heart to His will in my circumstances in that never-to-be-forgotten voyage, that

I felt I could go right back the same way if He had asked me.

"How painful it is to hear God's children say: 'I will not bear this,' or 'I will not have it so,' and make their own way of escape out of trial or difficulty. They thus lose the discipline, and often involve themselves in greater difficulties."

A few months after their arrival in America another little daughter was born, and Mr Fuller arrived to join them in the home land. Mrs Fuller took a cottage at North Chili, in New York State, and the family lived in the simplest manner, she performing all her domestic duties, and taking every opportunity to speak and write for India and its needs. Especially was she used among the students at the Free Methodist College at North Chili, under the care of Professor and Mrs Roberts. At conventions and camp meetings deep impressions were created.

Mrs Fuller was always self-denying in her dress. At one time in India there was considerable discussion as to whether the adoption of native dress by missionaries would or would not help them to get more in touch with the people, but Mrs Fuller thought it much more of a cross to dress like a poor European than to use the native dress. For missionaries to wear native costume did not commend itself to her mind and experience, although she sympathised with the motive.

Her simple dress was of course hopelessly out of fashion in America. The hat she was wearing, which passed well enough in India, caused a good deal of comment among her friends. Several times she essayed to buy a new one, but the hats seemed so fantastic and worldly she had no heart to buy. At one of the conventions a lady offered to accompany her to a shop and buy her a bonnet. "Something," she said, "restrained me that I had no liberty to go with her, though I could give no reason. Gradually the picture of a neat brown straw bonnet formed itself in my mind, and I often wished I might find one like it. After the convention we settled for the winter in a little village near a large city in Western New York. It was but a short ride into this city, where we did all our shopping. Soon after this a friend and I spent a busy day shopping, and just at the close she said: 'I have had five dollars given me to get you a bonnet, come and let us see about it.' Again I felt the same shrinking and said: 'It is too late, it is near train time; we will attend to it another day,' and as I spoke, my thought of a brown bonnet came again to me and I timidly added, 'I would like a brown straw bonnet.' My friend laughed and said, 'It is too late now to get a straw bonnet. They are all out of season.'

"On reaching home I found some letters on my table. In one of them was this paragraph: 'We are sending what you left here, and in the box we have put a brown straw bonnet, which Mrs R—— has sent you.'

"When the box came we opened it with great eagerness. There lay the bonnet. It was very pretty and a perfect realisation of the picture I had had. Never before or since have I had such comfort in a bonnet. It was the Lord's choice and provision for me. But above all was the precious lesson of His care and thought. Ever since, I have known in a deeper sense that our Heavenly Father knoweth that we have need of all these things, and that if we seek His kingdom first that He does add these things."

Since Mr and Mrs Fuller were in America before, the Christian Alliance had been formed under the leadership of Mr A. B. Simpson, of New York, and had commenced to create a strong missionary spirit among those who were attracted to its teaching. The watchword of the Alliance was the fourfold Gospel as indicated by the following motto:

"JESUS AS SAVIOUR, SANCTIFIER, HEALER, AND COMING KING."

Mr and Mrs Fuller attended the conventions of the Alliance and came in contact with its leaders. Before long the answer to their prayers for enlargement seemed to loom in sight. From the ranks of the Alliance, a band of missionary volunteers was called forth. Here were reinforcements for Berar, waiting a leader. Here were Mr and Mrs Fuller, trained and experienced missionaries, ready to welcome them and capable of leading them out and placing them in needy fields ripe for labourers, long prayed for.

Mrs Carrie Bates Rogers, writing of how the Lord raised up this large company of consecrated workers, says: "I have often thought of Jacob's saying, 'For with my staff I passed over this Jordan, and now I am become two bands' (Gen. xxxii. 10). When Mr and Mrs Fuller came out before, just one friend went to the steamer to see them off. They had one trunk and a satchel between them, and were obliged to stop in England till the Lord sent them more money to go on with. When they came out in the autumn of 1892 they had literally become two bands; Mrs Fuller leaving a month before her husband with seven new missionaries (five ladies and a married couple, Mr and Mrs Ramsey), and Mr Fuller coming on later with another married couple and a contingent of young men."

Evidently this new responsibility was not accepted without much prayer and seeking to know the mind of the Lord with regard to it. Mrs Fuller wrote concerning this period in America:

"God often has to repeat our lessons. After I had known rest of heart for a long time, and had proclaimed it to many, I came to circumstances where I had to make an important decision wherein the welfare of others depended upon what I chose. All unconsciously I began bearing the burden of the responsibility. I grew troubled and took up the old habit of sighing as I went about my work. It was a time when summer was merging into autumn, and the weather was often chill. I noticed as I took Baby Jean out that her cap was thin, and I would resolve to put a lining in it. But the resolve would be soon forgotten as other perplexities pressed in upon me.

"At last God spoke to my heart. One morning I awoke as usual troubled and under a cloud. I went down to the breakfast table saying, 'Oh, if I only knew what God wanted,' and hoping that the morning mail would bring me some token of His will.

"The mail came but there was nothing for me but a newspaper. With a feeling of disappointment I opened it carelessly, when lo, from the inside of the newspaper fell two soft, wadded, China silk baby cap-linings! What a halt there was in my soul! I stood like one God had rebuked. The rebuke was very real. God seemed to say, 'Why are you so troubled? If I, with the government of worlds upon my shoulders, can remember that your baby's cap needs a lining and can provide for it, can you not trust Me with your affairs?' How quickly I rolled the government upon His shoulders, and He did decide most wonderfully for us."

An incident must be related here which had an influence in God's ordering in calling some of these new missionaries into the field—a life sacrifice that bore much fruit. When Mr Fuller left Akola, an earnest young missionary from Ellichpur, Louisa Ranf, joined Miss Bates at Akola to assist in the work for a few months. Like others of these pioneer missionaries she also was much burdened in soul on account of the unevangelised country all about. Miss Ranf took charge of the boys in the orphanage and was a fountain of strength to the work. In November, 1891, she returned to Ellichpur on a short visit. On a Sunday afternoon she told her missionary friend at Ellichpur that she felt God had some great purpose in store for her, possibly to go to America and rouse missionary interest in the home churches for the great needs of India. When in prayer together a little later, she cast herself on the Lord in full consecration to fulfil His will, whatever it might cost her. That night she with the other missionaries at the station went to the English church at Ellichpur to attend the evening service. She knelt down and rising knocked her head against an oil lamp which fell and speedily ignited her thin dress. She was sadly burnt and died before midnight in spite of all that could be done. "Ah," she said, as she lay dying, "I know now what my prayer this afternoon meant." She realised that God had accepted the sacrifice and was taking her to Himself. She did not go to America to call out a band of workers, but the story of her consecrated life and almost martyr death did go, and was used to stir the fire of consecration in many hearts. I have myself met with several who said it was her death which led them to offer for India. Among them was one young man in the contingent that came out with Mr Fuller at this time.

Meetings to welcome these liberal reinforcements for the mission field were held in Bombay. Their advent seemed to bring a breath of fresh life into Christian circles in that city where they tarried for a few days before proceeding to Akola. Mrs Fuller especially seemed to have received a fresh inflow of spiritual life. At the service at the Grant Road Church on the Sabbath evening after her arrival, she told some of the experiences into which she had been led. She said she had been for some time in an unsatisfied condition, longing for an experience of holiness to which others testified, but which she seemed unable to grasp. While in this condition the words, "Christ in you, the hope of glory," were brought with great power to her soul. She saw then fully that Christ must sanctify as well as save, and that the power of an indwelling Christ was a grand thing to preach to the heathen. She felt that what the Lord wanted of His people was that they should let everything go, swing loose, go into bankruptcy of all their own strivings and efforts, and let the Lord Jesus take entire possession, speak through them, work through them and love sinners through them.

The same thought more amplified is found among her writings: "I was with some kind friends who were wholly given up to the Lord. During all my stay with them they never seemed to weary in ministering to me that I might have rest and comfort. I saw that I shrank from the sacrifice that they made to do it, and looking up queried: 'Lord, if it is right that they should do this, why do I shrink from it?'

"The answer seemed to come back: 'Child, you are wrong. You have your eye on them and the sacrifice. These dear ones are wholly

Mine. I can do through them what I please. It has been I caring for you through them.' I was filled with praise. I saw the possibilities of 'Christ in you' as I had never done before. It was not our imitating Jesus. It was not trying to reproduce the life of Jesus; but it was our being an empty surrendered temple for Jesus to dwell in, to repeat His own life in us.

"Our part is to keep the channels open and unobstructed. I saw how He would love sinners through us, and draw us out after them; how He would minister to them through us, and how He would pray through us. After that it was no longer the cry of my heart, 'Lord, help me to do this or that;' 'Lord, help me to speak;' and, 'How can I do that?' But as I met each emergency, it was, 'Lord, do this through me;' or, 'Lord, speak through me now,' and as I went to prayer I would abandon myself to Him to give the petition.

"I found, too, that Christ's presence in me often spoke to others without a word from me. Oh! the possibilities of such an abandoned life to God! Some of us have sweet happy flashes of this life, and how like a bit of heaven it is! Some of us see it, yet do not break away from old habits of thought about our being a wonderful Christian, and that God is going to help us do a great work. And so God can only work through us in a limited way. Yet His thought for us is that His life in us may be an abiding one."

CHAPTER VII

EXTENSION AND LANGUAGE DIFFICULTIES

"*Not by power, nor by might, but by My Spirit, saith the Lord.*"

IN accepting the position of Superintendents of the Alliance Mission in India, Mr and Mrs Fuller changed the method, though not the principle, of their life of faith. By the experience of the previous years they had proved that God could provide a table in the wilderness for those called to depend entirely on Him; and the basis arranged for the support of the Alliance missionaries commended itself to their experience and judgment, as a practical method of conducting a large work on the faith principle. No salaries were guaranteed to the workers, but a maintenance allowance was fixed, to be sent out monthly as supplies came in to the mission treasury in New York. When less than the full amount was in hand, allowances were to be paid in proportion. Mr and Mrs Fuller took no larger allowances than the most inexperienced recruit of the mission, and whenever there was shortage all shared alike.

Other detachments of new workers followed those who came out with Mr and Mrs Fuller, till, in the course of a year or two, the numbers swelled to fifty or sixty.[1] Then the visions of past years began to become realities. Stations were opened in populous parts of Berar, in centres for which workers had long been prayed for, and also in the adjoining territory of Khandeish, where the language spoken was also Marathi.

Parallel with this gratifying increase, a similar extension came to the work at Ellichpur and the hill district beyond. After fifteen years of hard, self-denying labour among the Kurkus (whose language he reduced to writing) Albert Norton[2] was invalided home to America in 1889. On his way thither he arranged for a new missionary agency in connection with Mrs Baxter's work at Bethshan, London, to take over his field of labour. Its early missionaries were received and initiated by Mrs Norton. After she joined her husband in America, Mr and Mrs Ernest F. Ward[3] (who had succeeded the Sibleys at Ellichpur) continued to help the new arrivals to settle in. But later, as those sent out from England increased in numbers and became acclimatised,

[1] In December, 1902, there were fifty-four missionaries on the field in nineteen stations, and eighteen at home on furlough.

[2] Now of the Boys' Christian Home, Dhond, Poona District.

[3] Working at present with "Vanguard Mission," Sanjan, Gujarat.

Mr and Mrs Ward left them in possession of the whole district, with Ellichpur as headquarters. This mission is now well established and is known as "The Kurku and Central Indian Hill Mission." Thus while workers from America were rapidly filling one part of the province of Berar, English Christians undertook the task of evangelising the other part.

"It is a marvel to me, Brother Fuller," said another experienced missionary whom he met in Bombay, "that you have been able to locate your men so quickly in all these places. We always find it most difficult to get a footing in a new place in our district, and when we do get the prospect of a house or a piece of land, the negotiations go on for months before we can come to any definite arrangement with these slippery land-owners. How have you done it?"

"I do not know," replied Mr Fuller, "except that we make every step a matter of prayer, and the Lord Himself goes before and opens doors."

When the needs of Berar were fairly provided for, Mr Fuller prospected in Gujarat, of which a large unmissioned district was opened up, and one which proved most fruitful and interesting as the birth-place of souls. Success came earlier than on the Marathi field, the people seemed easier to reach.

In all the continuous labour and planning which this work entailed, Mrs Fuller took her full share. If she was found resting in the hot weather, it was usually in a small house at Igatpuri, with a colony of young missionaries round her whom she was coaching in Marathi. Over and over again have I heard those whom she taught express their indebtedness to her for their proficiency in the language, the men as well as the women sharing her tuition.

Marathi is a beautiful and expressive language, but is also correspondingly difficult to acquire. A graphic account of the difficulties of its study was written by one of the ladies of the Alliance Mission, who was highly educated, having occupied a good position in a woman's college in America before offering herself for mission work in India. This lady, Miss M. Olmstead, said, "The language taxes the memory severely. After you have learned sixteen vowels and forty-eight consonants, you may be pardoned for supposing that you have the Marathi alphabet; but this is a vain hope. There are yet twelve vowel abbreviations and 131 principal compound consonants. It is an encouragement to know that these 207 characters make Marathi spelling very simple.

"Even to the Greek, Latin, and German scholar, Marathi inflections bring surprise. The noun has eight cases, the verb has four different methods of agreement, and seventeen, yes seventeen tenses, besides numerous verbal compounds.

"Marathi idioms are not only numerous, but often difficult to understand. The expression, 'having drunk the milk, throw it away,' means, 'drink the milk all up.' 'I sat watching his way,' is, 'I sat waiting for him.' 'Making thought comes to my soul,' is the Marathi way of saying, 'I can think.' When you have learned to say 'goose' and always think 'rat,' to use 'mice' for female buffalo, and 'dude' for milk, you are making progress, but more than that is required. Your previous notions of grammar must be sacrificed. You must sometimes view the instrument as the subject of the verb, and learn to say 'By God made created the world,' and 'God makes love on me.' . . . To learn Marathi easily, one needs to be simple, childlike, teachable. One needs the humility that is willing to learn from anyone; the unconsciousness of self that can make blunders and be corrected. This is the spirit so needful in entering the Kingdom of God and receiving the life more abundant. The study of Marathi is an admirable training school for missionary labour."

It is not easy to realise the difficulties that beset the path of the foreign missionary with such a language to face; and when it is remembered that the people's conceptions of God, of sin, the hereafter, etc., are so different from ours, the task of enlightening their minds would seem overwhelming but for the enablings of God's Holy Spirit. To encourage her pupils Mrs Fuller told of a crisis in her experience when she was abundantly helped to make her message clear. She said :

"In trying to lead our Christian people up to a full consecration, I saw that with all I said, they got no idea of a complete surrender to the will of God. One Saturday I was much burdened about it. I said to myself, 'Perhaps I do not use the correct Marathi words to express my thoughts.' I then prayed that I might be led to use the right words. The next morning, after an unusually good Sunday school, my husband announced that we would meet all who stayed for prayer. A number stayed, and as we knelt in prayer they began asking for the Holy Ghost. I felt they did not understand the very first step of separation and surrender. For a moment the old despair seized me, over the meagreness of my Marathi, but looking up to God, I broke in with the following question, 'What is the difference between a slave and a servant?' There were various answers, but the sum of it was, that a servant could remain in service or not, as he chose; but a slave was not supposed to have any will but his master's.

"What was said was simple enough, and but few words used, but the Spirit took the thought and multiplied it in their minds marvellously. One young man broke out in prayer, ' Lord, I've been Thy servant up to this time; I am Thy slave henceforward.' A woman cried out, ' Lord, give me the seal of my slave-ship, the Holy Ghost.' Another woman said in prayer, ' I've been a Christian a good many years, but I have never understood like this.' Then she followed this with a confession to another sister that her husband had stolen from her and she had covered it up. Two, who had not been speaking to one another, became reconciled. Some one then prayed in the language of the beautiful figure of the slave letting his master pierce his ear to the doorpost, 'that we might go out of the Lord's House no more for ever.'

" It was a wonderful meeting. Then the feeding of the five thousand was unfolded to me —Jesus bids us give this people to eat. Our knowledge of the language is limited, is like the five barley loaves and two fishes. Oh how we have been made to feel our insufficiency before this great multitude! But the Holy Ghost can take our words, and multiply and teach their meaning to those to whom we talk, and carry it beyond our expectation in results. Our sufficiency is of God."

CHAPTER VIII

THE BURDEN OF THE LORD: "MORE PRAYER FOR MISSIONS"

"*Always bearing about in the body the dying of the Lord Jesus, that the life also of Jesus might be manifest in our body.*"

It will be gathered by those who have followed the narrative thus far, that prayer was indeed Mrs Fuller's "vital breath." She prayed at all times, and under all circumstances, and watched and waited for the answers. She learned something of the value of prayer from Mr Finney, whose lecture on "prevailing prayer" was a trumpet call to the Church in his day. She found another example in one of her friends in America, already referred to, a woman in humble life, whom she spoke and wrote of, as her "praying friend, Mary Ann." This woman lived a life of constant intercession, and knew God as few of His servants do.

But it was on the occasion of a journey to America in 1894 that the importance of more prayer for missions was deeply impressed on

Mrs Fuller's heart, and focussed itself in a definite appeal to the Christians with whom she met in conventions and camp meetings. The object of her journey was some necessary consultation with the Board of the Alliance. Mrs Fuller was only absent from India for a few months, returning in the autumn with reinforcements for the Mission. In speaking about her journey on her return, she said she had not gone weighted with any concern to speak in public, nor with any burden of appeal for men or money. But looking to the LORD for guidance, she had been led out into work, and everywhere, and at all times, she was led to impress upon her hearers the great and universal need of MORE PRAYER FOR MISSIONS.

As she visited her old haunts in Northern Ohio, and stood by the grave of the sainted Finney, the same yearning desire filled her soul that the old time spirit of prevailing prayer might be revived. Addressing a convention of the Christian Alliance, she told her hearers: "God wants the prayer that reaches up to heaven, and brings the blessing down to earth. God wants you not to let go till the work is done. Some day you will find that God will charge the death of some missionary and the small success of many a work to His people at home. Remember our missionaries are young and inexperienced. They have the difficulties of acquiring the language, a vitiated moral atmosphere, and the power of Satan to contend with. May God lay upon your hearts the necessity of upholding them with your prayers." This earnest advocacy bore fruit in after years, and is still going on to bear fruit.[1] During this short furlough, Mrs Fuller received the most marked infilling of the Spirit that she had ever known, and from that time was more used of God than ever before.

Another point upon which Mrs Fuller's mind was much burdened at this time, and indeed to the close of her life, was the condition and possibilities of the Indian Christian Church. Speaking and writing on the necessity of prayer, Mrs Fuller said:

"Pray that God will thrust forth native labourers into the field. I feel this to be a deeper need than more European helpers. When I remember the history of this work in India, how it was founded in prayer, how two godly servants of Christ visited Ellichpur in this province, and, seeing its destitution, they spent New Year's day in prayer that God would thrust forth labourers into this field, and now He has called us all from all over the world—we represent seven different nationalities—and brought us here; I am deeply moved. When those friends prayed, many of us were unconverted. So I am moved to pray

[1] See Letters, etc. in Appendix.

for God to thrust forth an army of native helpers with us, many of whom are possibly now unconverted, but our God is able. The limitations to a missionary, of climate, of language, in being a foreigner, are great. One of their own people, baptised with the Spirit, must have greater possibilities than we. Pray that God will pour out His Spirit on the people, and that many may be prepared for His coming."

How Mrs Fuller longed and prayed for the deepening of spiritual life among the Indian Christians![1] She never missed an opportunity of influencing them, either as individuals or as a community. When, in 1895, the headquarters of the Alliance Mission in India were removed to Bombay, and Mr and Mrs Fuller took up their residence in that city, Indian Christians were continually flocking to her for advice and sympathy. They were always welcome to all the meetings at "Berachah" (as the Home in Bombay is called), whether held in English or Marathi, and many lives were

[1] This burden of prayer for Spirit baptised Christians to go forth as evangelists to their own people was taken up by others. May not the precious ingathering of souls which followed the rescue of famine waifs be in part the answer to these prayers? God's ways are not our ways. In judgment He sends pestilence and famine, but at the same time makes the affliction bear precious fruit to His glory. Twenty-five thousand waif children and widows were gathered in by missionaries and others during the famines of 1897-1900. The Gospel has had free course among these, and many are already going forth to tell the good news of Salvation.

brightened, and homes transformed, through her tender sympathy and loving counsel.

Here in Bombay Mrs Fuller's life was, if possible, more busy than ever. Their large house was continually filled with missionaries coming and going, besides several always in residence, studying the language, and carrying on work in the city.

It may have occurred to some that the Alliance was not needed in Bombay, where several large and important missionary societies had been established for many years. But it has been felt that God had a purpose in sending these new missionaries into the city at that time. Their immediate reason for taking a house in Bombay was the necessity of central headquarters; Bombay being conveniently situated between Berar and Gujarat, Mr and Mrs Fuller could more efficiently conduct the affairs of the Mission, and journey quickly to either place as needed.

Most of the missions already in the city had large educational work on their hands, and comparatively little attention was given to aggressive evangelistic effort. After missionaries had laboured in the city for seventy-five years, statistics showed that (in 1888) there were less than one thousand Protestant Indian Christians, including children.[1] This in a

[1] *Vide* paper read before the Bombay Missionary Conference, September 1888, by Mr Dhanjibhai Naoriji, the senior Indian minister in the city.

populace of 800,000, Bombay at that time claiming the position of the second city in the British empire as to population.

Bombay has always been looked upon as a hard field, and the Alliance, as well as other missions, found it so. On settling in the city, Mr Fuller at once organised a campaign of open air preaching. Every afternoon in the week, save Saturday, as soon as the heat of the sun cooled off, a party of men and women from the Alliance Home sallied forth to proclaim the Gospel, often joined by missionaries and lay Christians of various denominations. On Sundays they spoke in English to the crowds who frequented the seashore. On most other evenings they took up their stand in prominent places, where busy multitudes thronged the streets, and preached in the vernaculars.

This went on for about three years; meanwhile the plague broke out which has since carried off thousands of the population. It seemed as though God was speaking to the city through His servants; that many must have heard the truths of the Gospel at that time, who have since passed away, and who will be unable to say they had no offer of salvation, and had never heard the good tidings. There was doubtless some fruit to eternity in this labour, but there was also an open rejection of the claims of Christ. Especially were the English meetings on Sunday obstructed by a howling crowd of educated Hindus led on by a few bigoted Brahmins. On several occasions violence was resorted to, and speakers went home with wounds and bruises, literally "rejoicing that they were counted worthy to suffer" for Christ's sake. But their poor misguided assailants died like flies in the succeeding days of pestilence. That pestilence should follow the open rejection of God's proffered mercy and salvation, is but a fulfilment and repetition of truth reiterated in the Divine revelation. It was no accidental coincidence that the Alliance carried out that three years' proclamation of free grace for dying sinners. In May and June, 1896, ribald crowds jeered the preachers. In November and December and later, tens of thousands fled from the city; house after house was empty; twelve shops shut in one row of nineteen; and door after door bore the ugly plague mark with dates of deaths that had occurred. No one who went through those few months of the first outbreak of plague in Bombay will ever forget it. The death scenes all around, the unroofed houses, the fleeing multitudes, the terrified servants, the disappearance of familiar faces in the market and the shops. All cannot be told. The constant funeral processions growing more hurried and less elaborate day by day, the ambulance carts with their victims, the smell of disinfectants, the wailing of the mourning women, and the death-like emptiness of the streets after dark will live in the memory while memory lasts.

Mrs Fuller was herself only occasionally able to participate in the open-air work, but she helped and encouraged the other workers. One advantage she enjoyed of living in Bombay, was that she was able to keep her children with her longer than she could have done in a hot mofussil station like Akola. The elder ones made good progress in their studies by attending a Mission High School, while little Jean, the baby born in America, was the life and joy of her mother's heart, and her constant companion. A younger son had followed Jean, but he was early taken.

Jean was the sunshine of the house. She called all the missionary ladies "auntie." Her elder sister and brother George thought there was no one like Jean. She was a fairy-like child with dainty manners and quaint sayings. Her little heart turned to her mother's God like a flower to the sun. Once at an evangelistic mission in Bombay, when testimonies were being given at the closing meeting, Jean jumped from her seat by her mother's side and her childish voice rang out, "Those that seek Me early shall find Me."

More than once was Jean given back from the gates of death, so that her parents came to look upon her as given for the Lord's service.

One rainy season, Mr Fuller being absent from home, visiting the stations of the mission in China, Jean was taken sick and ran down completely. Her mother had to go to Akola on business, and took Jean, hoping the change would do her good, but she came back not so well. Sunday came and Mrs Fuller went to the open air meeting on the shore, but left as soon as she had spoken, and hurried home to put Jean to bed. She sat by her side weary and depressed. When the other workers returned it occurred to Mrs Fuller that though Jean's illness had been laid before the Lord for healing, they had not anointed her in accordance with James v. 14. As the oil was brought, Mrs Fuller said she felt a thrill of life go through her, bringing courage, hope and rest. Jean was anointed, with prayer, and slept soundly all night. In the morning she looked sweetly at her mother and said, "Mamma, I am well," and she was; not a trace of the disease returned after the anointing.

CHAPTER IX

TRAVEL AND BEREAVEMENT

"It is I, be not afraid."

WE speak of Mrs Fuller as living in Bombay at this time. She was; but how often we have called in at "Berachah" and found her absent in some distant part of the mission field, or just home from a journey, or about to start. The young missionaries placed out in these needy fields in Berar, Khandeish and Gujarat, enjoyed a motherly as well as a fatherly superintendence. In sicknesses, marriages, births and deaths, Mrs Fuller was ever at hand to help and sympathise. Every new station had its special history of trial and triumph in which she fully shared. How conscientiously she persevered in this frequent and arduous work may be gathered from her own account of her journeyings at one period, which I quote. (What she was to the missionaries she visited they will tell further on.)

"It was about the middle of March, the beginning of the hot season. I had been travelling much, and in a month had had ten nights of broken rest on trains. In some places I had spoken sometimes four hours a day. Then followed our first Marathi Convention, with the heavy sorrow of the first break in our ranks, and the death of precious workers. The Convention closed with much blessing, but the heat was becoming great, and at times I felt it much. I had visited all the stations in Berar but one, and wanted to visit this also before returning to Igatpuri. This station, Buldana, is off the railway, and the journey involved a six hours' ride in a tonga, facing the sun, in the hottest part of the day. It looked very tempting to go home and rest. My husband suggested that I write and say that I could not come. But what was I to write? That I was not able to come, and the heat was too great? Oh, no! I had long been off that ground. 'I can do all things through Christ who strengtheneth me.' The only thing that would satisfy me was to write that it was not God's will for me to come, and I kept feeling that it was!

"We left Akola on the early morning train. . . . We got off at Mulkapur and rested in the Travellers' Bungalow till noon, when the mail tonga should start. The heat was very oppressive, and I had to get between the doors for air so that I could breathe easily. How Satan contended with me that I dare not go; that to ride facing that sun in my weak condition might cost me my life. All that he said seemed so real and true. But blessed be God, there is such a thing as enduring, as seeing Him who is invisible. I knew it was not true. 'God is faithful that promised.'

"When the tonga came it was rickety and old, and the ponies were bad. One of them fell down on the way. How hot the sun was, and yet the words, 'The sun shall not smite thee,' stood out before me in living letters. They spread out over me like a great umbrella. The journey came to an end, and with it a warm welcome from our missionaries. I was not even weary. It was perfect victory. I would not have missed what faith brought out for me on that journey for any rest any place could have given me. I knew in a deeper sense than ever before what is meant by 'the life of Christ being manifest in my body.' I felt so well all my stay there, and reached home rested and refreshed. The spring of that victory remained in my life for weeks. Had I given up the journey and gone home to rest, I believe it would have taken several weeks to have got rested. It means much to have all our springs in God."

Mrs Fuller's journeyings in the Gospel were not confined to her own mission. She delighted to abound towards other fields also. An Indian pastor, who had profited spiritually by her ministrations in Bombay, besought her to come to his aid in impressing the truths of the Holy Spirit's work and office on his congregation in the Konkan, that part of the mainland lying behind the island of Bombay, below the mountain ranges called the Western Ghauts. It was not the distance but the difficulty of access which made the journey toilsome. Mrs Fuller went, and felt well repaid for the effort by the hungering and thirsting after the truth which she found among the people.

In January, 1897, she joined her husband and a friend in an evangelistic tour among the Syrian Christians in Travancore, in the extreme south of India. This involved a long journey by boat as well as rail, and an absence from home and children of several weeks. It was like a trip to another land—the people, their language and habits entirely different to those of Central India. The Syrian Christians are a sturdy race, the oldest body of Christians in India, dating back, it is said, from a visit of the Apostle Thomas, who, according to tradition, brought the Gospel to India and died near Madras.

Although much of the time sunk in indifferentism and brought under the papal yoke, there is now a hopeful reform movement among this interesting people. They have all these years preserved their autonomy, and manage their church affairs with a sturdy independence that is in refreshing contrast to some churches in other parts founded by modern missions. Mrs Fuller felt it was a new experience to be among these native brethren, who arranged all the details of the mission, and at whose invitation they were there. There was a great hunger to hear, even though the message came through an interpreter. The people would listen for five hours at a stretch, standing in the open air or sitting closely packed on the floor of the church. Mrs Fuller's own service was to have been confined to the women, but after she had once spoken in the open air the men crowded the verandahs of the church while she was speaking to the women inside. The accommodation was most primitive, and the travelling tedious, but they felt well repaid for all difficulties by the spirit of inquiry and interest in their hearers.

They had been away several weeks, out of the track of letters and telegrams, and as they turned their faces homeward a pang of depressing monition seized Mrs Fuller's heart with regard to Jean. She knew plague had been raging in Bombay, and that other complaints were rife there. Had her household been spared? When they reached the railway, letters met them, relieving her with the news that all was well, and on their arrival Jean was there to give her usual joyous welcome.

Arrangements had been made for Mr and

Mrs Fuller to take a furlough to America, starting in April. Lucia and George were to be placed at school, and would remain in America. But the mother's heart was perplexed about Jean. Not knowing of the struggle, Jeannie one day asked, "Mamma, will you leave me in America?" "I do not know, darling; do you want to stay?" was the reply. "Oh no, mamma; you go to America and leave George and Lucia, and I will stay here with Auntie Park till you come back." Jean accompanied her mother to the annual Marathi Convention, and also in her farewell visits to all the mission stations, and was so interested in the famine children, and ready to give them her toys and playthings. When at home she had a daily governess who taught her to read and write and sew, and taught her texts and hymns. Once in writing she was reproved that her letter "a's" were too narrow. She said they were "famine a's."

Jean's proposal to remain in India was not seriously considered. The rest must be told in her mother's own pathetic words: "At the Marathi Convention Jean came with beaming face and asked to be baptised with the new converts. But we thought best to put her off. How stupid we were! It might have meant much to her. In ten more days she was with Jesus. We reached home, glad our India journeys were all over, and hastened to complete the preparation for the long journey to America. Jeannie was full of glee about the home-going, and her near birthday when she would be six years old. On Monday afternoon we had a wedding in the house, and Jean looked a perfect picture as she watched the ceremony on a couch by herself, dressed in a dotted white muslin with blue ribbons. Five days later she lay in her coffin in the same dress, only we had changed the blue ribbons for white. She caught cold, and croup set in. On Friday evening she seemed better. Suddenly she grew restless and wanted to be carried, saying, 'I cannot sleep.'

"We carried her till we were all weary, and then the restlessness broke as suddenly as it came. 'Sing,' she said, in her sweet emphatic way. 'What shall we sing, darling?' we asked. 'Sing, "Praise Him, praise Him, Jesus our blessed Redeemer!"'

"But before we could sing she sang the first verse partly through. She listened quietly while we sang; then asked for the hymn, 'Jesus bids me shine.' When we had finished she again said, 'Sing.' We asked what she wanted, and she replied, 'Oh, Auntie Miller knows.' Mrs Miller[1] started, 'When He cometh, When He

[1] Mrs Miller, a Scotch member of the Alliance Mission, of whom Jean was very fond. She died twelve months later, and had a vision of Jean among the shining ones in her dying hours.

cometh to make up His jewels.' Several times Jeannie broke out in prayer. Once she said, 'O Lord, I do not like my voice like this; make it better.' And soon she spoke clearer, and recognised that Jesus had done it. Finally she asked that all might leave the room, and the light be put out. She was quiet as if asleep, when we noticed a change in her breathing. On bringing a light we found her unconscious. As the family gathered in the room she came to herself, and her eyes looked like stars, while her face wore an awed expression. She said one or two things, then looking at one of the ladies, said, 'Miss Park, Jesus' —— She never finished it. We repeated texts to her. As we watched her, something said to us, 'No more perplexity about her staying behind in the homeland.' Then came the words with power and comfort, 'Yet a little while, and He that shall come will come, and will not tarry' (Heb. x. 37).

"We repeated the words to Jean, and a little later she closed her eyes and 'fell asleep.' The anchor of the Word gripped us fast before the waves of sorrow poured over us. Yes, they which sleep in Jesus will God bring with Him. We do not wonder they called it the 'blessed hope,' and that Paul urged them to 'comfort one another with these words.' . . .

"We laid the precious dust in the English cemetery in Bombay. We gathered up her toys and sent most of them to the famine orphans as she would have desired. Her little outfit made for the homeland, untouched and unworn, was God's provision for two fatherless little girls on their way home too. How long was that journey, how tender the care He bestowed that our hearts were too dumb with sorrow to even ask for. Then He tenderly spoke one more word that had power to break sorrow. 'Blessed is he whosoever shall not be offended in Me' (Matt. xi. 6). Grief indulged becomes offence with God's dealing. 'If ye loved Me ye would rejoice' (John xiv. 28). Praise the Lord, but means, 'Thy will be done.'"

CHAPTER X

THE TIME OF INDIA'S TROUBLE

"*For the vision is yet for an appointed time, . . . wait for it, because it will surely come, it will not tarry.*"

THE pressing needs of India, then stricken with the weary famine conditions which have lasted more or less ever since, made Mrs Fuller's visit to America at this time a very busy one. She did not spare herself in going wherever she found an open door to tell of the starving thousands in their own district of Berar, and of the opportunities for service which lay before the missionaries who were left on the field. But while she was greatly in request for meetings and conventions, she took a little home for her children, and spent as much time as possible with them.

Mrs Fuller's own experience of the six famine girls she received in 1877, gave her an excellent leverage in advocating the cause of famine orphans now. She could tell of Shantibai, the elder one, mentioned before in these pages, now an earnest Christian woman, the efficient helper of a missionary engaged in gathering in famine children. Also of two others, Ashabai and Imambai, labouring in the same blessed work.

The "Story of Chandur" which Mrs Fuller wrote at this time may be suitably quoted here as a graphic delineation of missionary life in a period of famine:—

"In the farthest end of our Marathi field is the town of Chandur. It is not very large, but the centre of an extensive agricultural district, and many, many villages. When Mr Simpson was in India, he and Mr Fuller visited it, and decided to make it a mission station, and had it laid on their hearts to send Mr and Mrs Ramsey there. But there was not a house to dwell in, and we had no money in hand to build a house. And in addition, while this appointment was made, Mr and Mrs Ramsey were both very low with fever, and it was a question in the minds of those who watched over them whether they would ever live to go to Chandur. Was it the enemy contesting the appointment and the new station right in the heart of a place where he, alone, had ruled for centuries? We can never forget the fight of faith of that sick room. Jesus was victor! Praise His name! After a time of study they moved to a place as near Chandur as they could get, where a house was obtained, and lived on the borders of their field, sowing and preparing the soil of it with prayer as they completed their course of study.

"Then in a time of deep trial, God sent a love-token that He was with us, in the shape of a cheque for ten thousand rupees, just enough to put up three new houses, and thus permanently open three unoccupied fields. What joy it brought! And in Chandur was the first sod broken in all our mission field for a house.

"The little home was finished, and Mr and Mrs Ramsey and wee Sarah moved into it. Mrs Simmons and other ladies helped them there. After the joy of being in their own home and in their own station had had its first flush, the discovery dawned upon them that Chandur was not an easy field. There were no European comforts to be bought as in many other stations, for they were the only Europeans in the place. But that was as nothing compared to the constant rejection of the people. It was very hard. More than once has Mrs Ramsey and the young lady living with her been refused admittance to every house at which they called, and after a weary tramp have had to return home from what seemed a fruitless day's work. There were now and then baptisms in the other stations, tokens of life, drops of rain, forerunners of a shower; but no such tokens in Chandur. To the watchers there, there was only now and then the cloud as big as a man's hand that the wind soon chased away. The district around them was much like other districts, and was faithfully worked through the touring season.

"What battles with fever, too, have been fought in that little home! The station became known as one of the hardest in the mission. And it might also be called a bad town. But, oh, what seasons of prayer has the little home witnessed! 'Bethel' should many times have been written on its walls. In the midst of discouragement and trial was the vision of the flock God had given them. When Paul went to Corinth, the gay Paris of ancient times, after his seeming failure at Athens, he says he went in much fear and trembling. And when it seemed as if the history of his stay in Athens was to be repeated in Corinth, God said to him, 'Be not afraid, but speak; and hold not thy peace; for I am with thee, and no man shall set on thee to hurt thee; for I have much people in this city.' And who were they? The mighty and noble of the city? No. 'Not many mighty, not many noble,' but there were some, and the rest were slaves, pickpockets, evil men, Shylocks extorting money, idolaters and men out of the very scum of Corinth, for he writes, 'Be not deceived; neither fornicators, nor idolaters, nor adulterers, nor effeminate, nor abusers of themselves with mankind, nor thieves, nor covetous, nor drunkards, nor revilers, nor extortioners, shall inherit the kingdom of God. And such were some of you; but ye are washed, but ye are sanctified, but ye are justified in the name of the Lord Jesus and by the Spirit of our God.'

"God gave Paul the vision, and then fulfilled it. God gave our dear workers in Chandur the vision of a church, and it was yet to be transformed out of the very scum of the populace about them perhaps, and out of some of the noble, for, thank God, though it does say, 'not many wise men after the flesh . . . not many noble,' yet it does not say, 'not any.'

"Time wore on. Then God took little prattling Sarah, and how still the mission house was. Loving hands from another station fashioned a coffin out of the shelves of a cupboard, and covered it with white cloth. There was no beautiful cemetery, green and well cared for, to lay the precious dust away in to await the great trump. But the headman of the town gave them a place on top of a rocky hill. What a world of pathos there is in these lonely, solitary graves in India, the Congo, and Soudan! It was a heavy blow, but better fitted the workers for the place God had given them. Henceforth, in our own minds, the station became 'the station with the grave on the hill.'

"Then came the famine, and it was first

heaviest at Chandur, of all our stations. It found Mr and Mrs Ramsey worn, and it was the beginning of the hot season, when we had planned that they should both have a thorough rest and change at the hills. But as the need grew greater, after much prayer, they were able to touch the spring of His life for theirs, and went on, under great pressure of work, through the heat. Early God gave them a soul, in the clear conversion of a famine refugee. He had been an opium smoker and a slave to its use. The doctor told him it might mean death to break it off at once. The missionaries told him Jesus was able to heal. The man fought the battle out himself, and launched out upon Jesus, and never had any trouble whatever, and through it Jesus was made real to him. He was baptised at our Marathi Convention (at Akola). As he went down into the water, Miss Olmstead, with beaming face, turned to me and said in Marathi, as she pointed to the man, 'Chandur's first fruits.'

"Will the early missionaries in the Marathi field ever forget the baptisms of our first converts in the beautiful river at Akola, with the setting sun gilding the water, the heads of the workers, and filling all the trees with its glory? It seems to us we can yet hear the music of the Marathi hymns as they were wafted over the water.

. . . . .

"We pass over the weary months of famine suffering, the epidemic of cholera that came as the rains came on, of God's deliverance, of the days of pressure and work, and let Mrs Ramsey's letter finish our story:—

"'These are very busy days with us, and God gives strength for the day. Since we received Mr Lambert's load of grain we have seen, oh, so much sadness and hunger. We thought it bad enough before, but the news of the grain must have spread like wildfire, for crowds began to come from the villages, eight and ten miles away. Poor things! instead of stomachs they had loose flaps of skin covering them.[1]

"'Saturday we had twenty-one hundred, some of them representing a family of six or seven. We had given out tickets, but there was so much imposition we took them back, and gave equally to all. To-day we must have had two thousand in all. Besides this there are numbers of fresh arrivals daily, pleading and falling at our feet for food. We have felt that we could not keep up the rush without some solid rest. Sometimes it has been short in the middle of the day, but last Sunday Mrs Simmons just ordered that no

[1] The Mennonite Church in America sent out a large quantity of corn, which was disbursed through missionaries, by Mr George Lambert, their delegated almoner, who visited India for the purpose.

one should be allowed in the compound, and the quiet day was very refreshing.

"'The past week has been wonderful in its experience. One wonders where all the emaciated forms come from; but as we visit the villages we find that most of the people live on the green leaves they can pick up anywhere, and some have the luxury of a couple of pice a day for weeding. To such families even a seer (two pounds) of grain means much.

"'You know how the children look with stomachs distended almost ready to burst, not even the form of hips, large heads and shrunken limbs. And, oh! what vermin and filth! You may fancy what a place would be like after two thousand had been sitting on it. We refused grain one day until they had cleaned the place.

"'Coming thus in contact with the people, one sees their need as fellow beings, and feels for them. But I have come to the conclusion that great as is their physical need in this awful time, it is only an index to their deeper need. What deception, lying and rascality one sees daily for a mouthful of food! I do hope as you hold up the one need of food to the dear ones in the homeland, that they may never fail to take in the fact that these dear people are dying without a Saviour. We often groan as we fail to see deep conviction of sin that would make them cry out, "What shall we do to be saved?"

"'I went through the Poor-house yesterday. I saw fourteen men and women lying on cots in the last stages of starvation. The word "skeletons" does not express the sight. Only one had strength enough to complain.

"'Mrs Simmons took nine boys to the Akola Orphanage to-day. I wish I could give the history of each. One was lying on the ground unable to walk after the distribution of grain one morning. With great tears rolling down his face he said, "I have nobody. If I had my father he would care for me, but he is dead." He is still with us. One boy has his baby brother, whom he cares for like a mother. My heart aches over them all. What should we do if we had no means to help them?

"'And now I know you will rejoice with us to hear that we have had our first baptism in Chandur. Last Saturday we baptised eight persons. You can imagine our joy as we rode to the river. Dear Mrs Simmons and I took one another's hands, and said we would rather be here than in any place in the world.'

"After many days has the vision begun to be fulfilled, and a little church has been formed on Chandur's hard soil. Its foundation was laid in prayers, and tears, and trust, in the days of cloud and darkness. We rejoice with them. A few mails before these same hearts had written us: 'Sometimes we have high hopes of some, and again they are dashed to the ground. But whether we see any fruit or not, may God help us to stand.'

"When a missionary enters a city and district, there are hearts that are sore with bereavement, heavy with discipline, trial and disappointment, with a hunger that no pilgrimage, vow, penance or austerity has ever satisfied, longing for something, and that something is Jesus, of whom the missionary alone can tell. Let us pray that he may find such hearts. Perhaps that drunkard rolling from one side of the street to the other that he meets; that debauchee with his ribald song; that bold-faced woman who peers so shamelessly into his face; that thief who stole the blanket out of his cart while he was preaching in the market-place; that thin-visaged money-lender exacting his pound of flesh from that poor mother and her children; that elderly Brahmin who passed him so haughtily just now, or those young high caste boys just out of high school, who held up his mistakes in Marathi for ridicule to the crowd as he preached, and battered him with foolish questions to no profit; perhaps these are the very ones that God has in that city to transform, who are to be the future church—and to whom it shall be written: 'And such were some of you, but ye are washed.'

"God grant that the friends at home who support the missionary may catch with him 'the vision,' and though it tarry, wait with him for it until it be fulfilled, 'because it will surely come, it will not tarry.'"

While Mr and Mrs Fuller were travelling about in America and Canada, pleading the needs of India, their own circumstances were not luxurious, except as they might be here and there entertained in homes of luxury. For herself the simplest fare and entertainment satisfied Mrs Fuller; it was only for her children that she now and then sighed for the means to give them some little extra indulgence. A little story she wrote concerning this period was entitled "OUR ONLY THANKSGIVING TURKEY."

"As it neared Thanksgiving Day, we remembered we had never had a real home Thanksgiving in our little family, and there came a desire to have one, and we almost choked as we remembered that it would not only be our first one, but might be our last one together. We well knew in parting with our children, the circle might never be complete again.

"As the desire grew, I began wondering if I could afford a turkey, and have a real old-fashioned Thanksgiving dinner. For years I have known the secret that nothing is too small for Jesus, and that He withholds nothing that is best for us. I did not feel at liberty to spend the money, but I left it to Him to provide if He saw best for us to have it. So one day at the table I said, 'Children, I am asking the Lord for a Thanksgiving turkey.' The suggestion was met with a round of applause.

"Just the week before Thanksgiving, I was asked to assist in some meetings in Canada. I went very reluctantly, with the promise that I should be allowed to come back the evening before Thanksgiving. Just as I was leaving, a feeling of misgiving seized me. 'What if God should not send the turkey? The children will be disappointed. There is no promise in the Bible where you can demand a turkey. If He gives one, it will be pure grace from beginning to end.' Then I said, cautiously, to the children the day I left: 'I'll be home sure in time for Thanksgiving, and if there is no turkey, I know we can afford a fowl.' 'Oh,' screamed my boy in reply, 'Mamma, do not let your faith down to chicken!' I responded as brightly as I could, and said before leaving for the train: 'Well, if any letters come bearing a Turkish post-mark you may open them.'

"My heart was soon absorbed in the meetings, but I did not forget the dear children at home, and now and then reminded the Father about the turkey. Finally the week was over, and the homeward journey had begun. I had had one bright letter from the children to which they had added that as yet there had been no news from Turkey!

"It was very cold and snow was on the ground. I broke my journey at one place, and drove four miles in the cold and over bad roads, to see some dear friends whom I might not see again. It cost me some self-denial, for I was eager to get home. But I felt amply repaid with the royal welcome they gave me.

"As we went into the dining-room for dinner soon after my arrivai, my friend put her arm about me and said: 'We have had a family council to-day over whether we should have turkey to-night or fowl: and we decided to have fowl and give you the turkey to take home with you!' It may seem a trifle to some of my readers, but I bowed my heart in gratitude to God. They had not known a syllable of our desire, and had only acted as the Father had led. *He* knew, and that should always be enough for our hearts.

"The next morning I saw I was going to be delayed one train in getting home, so I telegraphed the children to keep them from being disappointed, and added to the telegram, 'Good news from Turkey.'

"It was a royal Thanksgiving day. We kept the key turned on 'our skeleton in the cupboard'—that it would probably be our last Thanksgiving together—and would not think of it. I never tasted such a turkey. It was perfect. A dear friend who was with us said to me, 'How sweet it is to be fed from the Lord's hands.' Surely it was His love and care that sweetened it all and gave flavour to our meal, and our trust was renewed in His love and care. Truly God delighteth in mercy."

The foreboding that this would be the last Thanksgiving they as a family would celebrate was destined to be fulfilled. The next year Mrs Fuller was in India, and when the following anniversary came round she had joined her darling Jean in the true Homeland where it is all Thanksgiving.

CHAPTER XI

LITERARY WORK IN AMERICA AND INDIA

"*As poor, yet making many rich, as having nothing, yet possessing all things.*"

MRS FULLER'S facile pen was busy in intervals of leisure during this visit to the home country. From time to time she had contributed incidents in her own experience to the press, particularly to the weekly Christian paper published by the Christian and Missionary Alliance. She now edited, and added to them, for publication in a little volume under the title, "God's Care."[1] (By permission many of these incidents have been incorporated in this story of her life.) In these she traced the loving over-ruling care of God in the smaller as well as in the more important concerns of life; of times when she had been comforted in trouble, helped in difficulty, or guided in the journey of life. In all she magnified the grace and power of God.

In March of the following year, 1898, Mrs Fuller was back again in Bombay, welcomed

[1] Published by the Christian and Missionary Alliance, 692 Eighth Avenue, New York.

by many friends, and soon took up her old manner of life, saving that her journeys up country were rather less frequent, as the new missionaries were gaining their own footing and required less oversight. This, with the absence of her children, gave her more leisure to use her pen, and in this manner utilise a sacred talent in the Master's service. For years she had published an occasional paper giving tidings of the mission to friends at a distance, and which circulated chiefly, though not wholly, in America. But now a wide opportunity offered for influencing the missionary and Christian public in India outside as well as inside her own circle. In this connection it is necessary to allude to personal matters of the compiler of this narrative.

For more than ten years my husband, Alfred S. Dyer, had been in charge of the *Bombay Guardian*, a Christian weekly newspaper in Bombay, circulating throughout the whole of India. The condition of his health made it imperative that he should rest, and as time went on it was clear that his work in that position was finished. In July, 1898, two of the Alliance missionaries, Mr and Mrs Wm. Franklin, took charge of the paper and enabled us to get away for a change. The next month Mr and Mrs Fuller relieved these friends, and helped us more or less throughout the remainder of the year, Mrs Fuller giving a considerable portion of her time to the work. It was our desire that they should take the responsibility of the paper on our leaving India. They were willing to do this, and for Mrs Fuller to make it her main work if the Lord willed it so. But eventually it was evident that this was not the case. The Lord provided for the *Bombay Guardian* in other ways. But during the remainder of her life, Mrs Fuller continued her contributions to the paper, and helped and encouraged the younger workers, Mr and Mrs F. Percy Horne, upon whom the work devolved, and who at the time of writing are still bravely carrying it forward.

It was in connection with the *Bombay Guardian* that Mrs Fuller's most valuable literary work was performed. During her lengthy missionary experience, the wrongs suffered by India's women had burnt into her soul, and her friendship with Pandita Ramabai had given her a further view behind the curtain of caste and custom that hides so much of this suffering from the outer world. She conceived the thought of a series of papers on this subject for the *Bombay Guardian*, and having set herself to the task, threw all her energies into it. She felt deeply the responsibility she had undertaken, and took the utmost pains to verify every fact she stated. In her quest for correct information she interviewed Hindus, Mahomedans and Parsees, consulted libraries, hunted up ancient and modern authorities, and took journeys to North India and other distant points. She abjured generalities, and accepted no statement as a fact until she had it from two or three separate sources. The result was one of the most valuable works yet published, covering the entire subject indicated by the title, "The Wrongs of Indian Womanhood."

In the commencement she pictured an educated Hindu youth, who had graduated at Oxford or Cambridge, and moved freely in English family life, returning to his own land, the contrast he would find, and the disappointments that awaited him in the society of his sisters and mother, and of the girl destined to be his wife. Here she showed the wrong to Indian society generally by the absence of education for women. But she went on to deeper and more serious wrongs, and dealt with the evils of child marriage, enforced widowhood, prostitution in the name of religion, nautch girls, temple women, and that cruellest wrong of all, the marriage of girl children to the god Khandoba. These chapters excited much interest in India, and the desire was expressed that they should be published in permanent form, which was afterwards done.[1]

[1] "The Wrongs of Indian Womanhood," by Mrs Marcus B. Fuller. Chicago: The Fleming H. Revell Co.; Edinburgh and London: Oliphant, Anderson & Ferrier.

Mrs Fuller's ready sympathy for all in trouble led her to be frequently consulted by parents in regard to children who might be causing them anxiety. To meet such cases she wrote a little paper called, "Covenant Promises to Parents," showing from the Scriptures what promises Christian parents can lay hold of on behalf of the salvation of their children, concluding with the wider outlook that Christian parents should claim such blessings, in order that their children should be made a blessing; in fulfilment of the promise that in the seed of Jesus Christ all the families of the earth should be blessed. This is so valuable that we give it in the Appendix *in extenso.*

Another subject with which she dealt faithfully in the columns of the *Bombay Guardian* embodied a sorely needed warning. She felt that somehow money had come to have too prominent a place in mission work, that there were too many paid agents and too few volunteer workers among the Indian Christians. She longed to see men and women filled with the Spirit, and called to the work of witnessing for Christ, while earning their living by secular employment, or if giving their whole time to the work, to see them supported as far as possible by their Indian brethren, and willing to live in the humblest fashion, as a testimony that they were not preaching for worldly gain.

She wrote tenderly as well as faithfully upon this topic.

Mrs Fuller rejoiced greatly over the progress of Pandita Ramabai's work on the lines here laid down. When Ramabai returned from America in 1898 without any guaranteed financial backing for the new developments of her work at Mukti, Mrs Fuller was happy in the fact. She wrote: "Ramabai landed in India with no money, and has now no promises for her mission save the promises of God. We can only say we are glad of it. It is the witness the Indian church needs. Had she come back with a large sum of money, it would have turned the eyes of the Indian church to America and England as the source of help for work, but now she can by her testimony turn them to God."

The fact cannot be too much reiterated that all through Mrs Fuller's own life she lived what she taught. It was not an unfrequent experience to her to be out of money. On one such occasion, when pestered by a European loafer for help (a class of which there are many in Bombay), she had to reply, like Peter and John, "Silver and gold have I none, but such as I have give I thee," and went on to testify from her personal experience that God was able to supply all need in answer to prayer. The man persisted in assuring her that God had sent him to her for assistance. "Well," she replied, "if that is true, God knew I had no money, so did not send you to me for that; but He must have sent you to me for what I could give you—my testimony. I do not see but what you will have to take that." At that his face cleared, and thanking her for her words, left.

When the late Editor of the *Bombay Guardian* was leaving India, there was a writing-desk in his possession, which it was not convenient to take back to England. It was a good desk, with drawers to the ground on either side. As it had been the gift of a dear friend, and had sacred associations attached to it, he felt he would like it to continue to be used in the Lord's service. The thought came to give it to Mrs Fuller, who was just then engrossed in her articles on "The Wrongs of Indian Womanhood."

A note was written, and without giving her any notice the desk was despatched to her home on the heads of two or three coolies. She returned a little note of thanks, which touchingly indicated the self-denial of her life. She said she had often longed for such a desk, but had never felt able to purchase one. When the men walked in with it and she realised that it was God's gift to her, she was moved to tears of thanksgiving and joy, and her heart filled with praise to the giver of all good gifts.

It will always be a pleasant memory that the farewell meeting given us when leaving Bombay in 1899, with its messages of hope and encouragement for the future, was held in the home of Mr and Mrs Fuller. Several valued friends and fellow-workers then with us have been called Home, but how little we or she thought that her life journey was so nearly ended.

Mrs Fuller was never more active in public life in Bombay than at this time. She was in constant request for meetings and Bible readings, both in English and Marathi. She joined heartily in open air meetings at the bandstand, the evening resort of European "society" in Bombay. God owned her testimony there to at least one soul, who told after her death, of the blessing received. To how many more it came as a message from God, eternity will reveal. It required some courage to enter that circle of fashion, with carriages by the dozen drawn up around the fence, filled mostly with the worldly and careless.

Mrs Fuller sometimes had visions of an organised city mission to the fallen of both sexes in Bombay, to be called the "Jeannie Mission," after her sainted little daughter. It was not God's thought for her, but may He not through her be calling some other to stand in the breach in this awful need? Her spirit was stirred to its deepest depths by the flagrant and open manifestations of immorality in the city, and one of her last efforts was to endeavour to deepen the sense of responsibility in the hearts of Bombay Christians in this respect, and to urge to some adequate attempt to cope with the prevailing sin in God's name, for His glory, and the protection of the young of both sexes who are inevitably exposed to the contaminating influence of this evil. To this end she spoke and wrote, and interviewed representative men and women. God granted her a measure of success, but such witnessing is still a crying need in Bombay.

CHAPTER XII

THROUGH DARK DAYS TO EVERLASTING LIFE

> "*When thou passest through the waters*
> *I will be with thee.*"

IN October, 1899, dark clouds of famine again spread over Western India, affecting all the mission stations of the Alliance. Mrs Fuller was henceforth entirely engrossed by the immensity of this need. After having, with her husband, made a survey of the field, she returned to Bombay and wrote an eloquent and touching appeal to friends in the home lands. A few extracts from this letter will give an affecting picture of the conditions with which this Mission—together with all others in the area of Western India—was confronted. Mrs Fuller wrote :—

"Hitherto when famine has been visited upon India, years have elapsed before another has come. Three years ago the famine that we passed through was very sore, yet when the rains came in 1898, we drew our breath freely and rejoiced in what seemed returning prosperity to this afflicted land. Millions had died, thousands of homes had been broken up for ever, thousands of hearts had been bitterly bereaved of all, yet as soon as the cloud lifted, and the first rays of prosperity began to dawn, millions of people went back to their idols, forgetful of the hand of God that had been on them, unbroken and unhumbled by their awful trial. 1898 passed away, and the hot season of this year was drawing to a close. The rain burst as usual, and in some parts of the country fell freely, but in others the clouds soon rolled back, and with the exception of occasional showers, no more fell. Clouds came only to be driven over our heads by the wind, without watering the earth. The papers kept predicting that if rain came within a certain period, the crops would be saved. But sufficient rain never came. The monsoon is practically over, and the looked for rain has not fallen; the tender shoots of the second crop are yellowing, and will soon be burned up. Never in any land has the constant bright sunshine been so unwelcome, or so mocking as in the last two months, and the cloud of famine, that at first was no bigger than a man's hand, has grown and spread till at last the beginning of another awful visitation is again upon a large part of this beautiful land.

"At first I felt it could not be; that the outlook had been exaggerated; but a trip of three weeks through Gujarat and Berar, our own mission field, has proved it to be all too true, and appalled our hearts with the prospect of the coming days. As we passed through Berar the other night on our homeward journey, the fields and land on either side lay flooded with the soft light of the new moon. Here and there we could see the light of some village. We were deeply moved as we thought of the suffering and anguish the same moon would witness on its returns in the next few months.

"As you know, our work is in two fields, in which we have sixteen stations. Five of these are in Gujarat, and eleven in the Marathi country, in the provinces of Berar and Khandeish. The famine is closing in sharply in Gujarat. In our most northerly station, Viramgaon, not a drop of rain has fallen since June 26th. Cattle have been dying in large numbers. Gujarat is a rich, hitherto prosperous province, that has not known famine for well on to a hundred years. We have already received a number of orphans into our two orphanages, which I fear will be but an earnest of more to come. At Kaira a little child was found thrown away in the river bed, and is now doing well in our girls' orphanage. Sad as the tokens of distress are that are daily multiplying about us, they but foreshadow coming days when the distress will be many fold more.

"In Berar I found the out-look intensified

by a sore water famine. There has been a shortage in the rainfall for several years. Last year the water level was declared to have sunk ten feet below the normal level. As no rain in the natural course of events can be expected till next June, the out-look for man and beast is appalling. Some villages where wells have failed are already deserted, and as I left the province we heard of the outbreak of cholera in several villages. Buldana, Khamgaon and Amraoti are the most affected by the scarcity of water of all our stations. Dear Miss Yoder, with her large family of orphans, has been in great straits for water. The mission well now only produces a few buckets of water each day for drinking purposes, but for the school she has to cart water. She cannot bring enough for washing the girls' clothes and their baths, so every Saturday A.M. at four o'clock she takes the whole school to a stream three miles away. Some of the people have said to them, 'You say the famine is sent because of our sins and idolatry, now what have *you* done that you have no water?' While they were praying for direction, a letter brought $35 from Mr Egley in Indiana, which they took as an earnest for enough to dig a new well. Other gifts speedily followed, and men at famine wages were employed. They got down twenty, twenty-five feet, and no water. A few days later they struck a stream of running water which for a time hindered the blasting. May it indeed prove a permanent flow—a lasting witness between those who believe the *Living God* and those who do not. God has promised that our bread and water shall be sure, and we never realised it so fully as now.

"Oh the awful suffering that the next few months will witness! At Christmastide, dear friends, as you thread the streets lined with gay shops, as you buy presents for those who have no need, as you lavish money on costly entertainments and luxurious feasts, would that I had the power to lift space and let you witness the awful pinch and hunger and suffering that millions of *fellow*-beings will be suffering at the same time. Bear ye no responsibility, or shall the vision fade away like a will-o'-the-wisp, and you press on in comfort and luxury? How will it sound as the Master says in eternity, referring to this same holiday season,—'I was a hungered, athirst, and naked, and ye heeded not?'

"We have decided to take all orphans that are brought to us without regard to number, and trust God for future guidance and help with them; to take the children of destitute widows, and of widowers who cannot work on relief work, and care for their children, and then at the close of the famine, return them to the parents, and in this way keep families together. We desire to help young women and widows to work, and tide them through the famine without their moral ruin, hoping to start some industrial scheme so that some of the women can earn their way. Beside suffering and death, a famine is a great calamity to the people in many ways, they get mendicant habits, families get broken up, while to say the least, it is demoralising for people to leave their homes and villages, and herd in Poor-houses and on big Relief Works. Before the people get emaciated and reduced beyond the power to work, is the time to help, but all our schemes require money to put them in execution, and out of our own means we are unable to do it. *We wish to give as little gratuitous help as possible.* . . .

"And last we beg constant prayer. Humanly speaking there is a heavy year before India with the plague and famine. May prayer not be made that the people may humble themselves under the mighty hand of God, and turn to Him in large numbers? that hundreds may not escape the lesson this time? Also that the missionary may be fitted for the hour and opportunity before him: that he may know how to bring the people face to face with God; that he may be sustained in health and kept from the epidemics that are sure to follow. We lost one beautiful missionary last famine by cholera. Remember us in prayer."

This letter was followed by two others giving details of the work as it was accomplished. The first bore good fruit. Over Rs. 10,000 were received for famine relief in February 1900, and nearly as much in January. But the pressure on time and strength, to Mrs Fuller especially, became more and more severe. Some extracts from her third famine letter, which was her last, are intensely pathetic. After thanking her friends for the noble and generous help they had rendered, she gave statistics to show that that famine was the worst with which India had been affected since it came under British rule, and told how the money sent was being used on the lines laid down in the previous letters.

"Two of our ladies found a child thrown away in the fields, and again the same ladies found a little girl thrown in a thorn hedge. You will find her in the orphanage with her head still bound up from the wounds the thorns made. Mr Andrews and I found a little girl deserted by the roadside, so stiff with cold that we thought her at first dead or dying. We had nothing to put around her to warm her. She was dirty and had vermin on her, and I must confess that for a second it cost a struggle before I could wind my dress skirt around her and let her share the cape I wore. Mr Andrews found a woman apparently dying under the bridge in the city. She had two beautiful children, that she begged Mr Andrews to take. To their great surprise she came to the house the next day, a little better. By degrees her timidity wore off and she came to stay. She was a gentle, sweet-tempered woman. I said to her playfully, 'I suppose you will be running away soon.' 'Oh no,' came the reply, '*I have come home!*' And it was a home-coming in a double sense, for not only was she cared for by loving hearts as a sister, but she seemed to accept Christ and thus find an Eternal Home. She gradually failed, and in dying whispered to Mr Andrews, 'Take care of my children.'

"The strain is yet a long one before us. How dark the prospect for help looked in the beginning, I cannot tell you. It would look dark yet save for the promises, and we know we shall not be tempted above that we are able.

"The famine in Gujarat was two months ahead of Berar and Khandeish in severity, but now the pinch there grows harder daily. But the well at Khamgaon which we dug has up to date given an abundant supply of water to the orphanage.

"By the time this letter reaches you, dear friends, the great heat of the hot season will have begun, and we beg much prayer from you all for our devoted missionaries, very few of whom will get away to the hills for much needed rest. Some of them were hardly rested from last famine, and have their furlough home due. Will you be faithful to pray for them? We now have fourteen mission stations involved in famine. There is also the danger of epidemics at the relief works. Near Buldana recently in one camp thirty people died in four hours of cholera. In Gujarat there is an epidemic of measles. The cold of the winter, contrary to all expectations, has been very severe, and influenza in some parts has prevailed. Small-pox is breaking out in many sections.

"We have had a sore time in Bombay. In seven weeks the whole number of deaths in the city rose to 14,673; as the normal death-rate of the city at its highest is only 500 per week, you can see how sore this has been. Beside plague, small-pox broke out, and in these seven weeks 1,308 deaths came from this dreadful disease. There were said to be at one time 100,000 famine refugees in the city, which no doubt made matters much worse. And now a hush falls upon me, and my pen moves more slowly as I tell you that our precious Miss Park, who has been such a stay and help to us in the Bombay Home for five years, has fallen asleep. She contracted small-pox, probably as she went about her work in the city. In fact none of us can run away from it. Hers took the confluent form and early manifested fatal symptoms. Need I tell you, dear friends, what a sorrow it has been, and for a little the sun seemed darkened, but Jesus has given the oil of joy for mourning, and the garment of praise for a spirit of heaviness, and we are glad for her whose work was thus so early finished. She laboured largely among the Jews in the city.

"And now again I beg prayer, that God may keep your beloved missionaries, and that His will may be fully wrought out in this heavy judgment. Never before in the many years I have been in India have I faced so dark an hour. Never before perhaps have I been more hopeful. God is at work. It took ten judgments on the rich, prosperous land of Egypt before they heard God's voice. Pray that we His servants may keep above it all, working in fellowship with God, until righteousness come to many thousands. Pray, *pray*, PRAY, dear friends, for dear India, as you have never prayed before. He reigns. His purposes for this great idolatrous land are ripening fast. And pray for us and forget not our need. 'Whatsoever He saith unto you, do it.'"

This weighty message was a fitting close to a life of service for the Lord. Before it reached the friends in America, to whom it was mainly addressed, its writer was laid low. She suffered severely from an attack of influenza, and felt much worn and very weary, and was hoping to be able to take a little rest. But cholera broke out in Khamgaon, some of the missionaries were attacked, and Mrs Fuller put her own feelings aside, and went to their relief. In her enfeebled condition she took the infection, and was brought to the gates of death. At one time she was thought to be dying, but rallied, and was taken to Bombay, where every loving care was bestowed upon her. But lung and heart complications ensued, followed by dropsy, and she lingered, only to suffer. For many years Mrs Fuller had known the Lord as her healer, and had given many precious testimonies to His power over the human body, manifested in answer to prayer. But, during this sickness, she said she was "unable to touch God for healing." She lived thirteen weeks after the attack of cholera at Khamgaon. At times her husband and other watching friends felt hopeful that her life would be spared, but this was not to be. The Lord saw best to take her to Himself. Her life work was finished, and she was glad to be "with Christ, which is far better." Her tired body was laid to rest amid the luxuriant verdure of the tropics, in the lovely Sewree Cemetery. Grief at her loss was sincere and widespread. Every Protestant mission in Bombay was represented at her funeral. European and Indian Christian young men shared the privilege of carrying her body to its last resting place, there to remain only "Till He come."

. . . . . .

Tributes to her memory poured in from all classes in India. Extracts from letters and testimonies of personal friends are given in the following chapter. Among those printed in newspapers, one or two may be specially mentioned. The *Y.M.C.A. Monthly* of Bombay said: "It is not given to many women to exercise a strong hold over young men, but when the announcement was made that Mrs Fuller would speak at a young men's meeting, not only was no incongruity felt, but a good meeting was confidently anticipated. Her transparent earnestness constrained the attention, attracted by the transparent ease and fluency of her diction, impressed with the reasonableness of her thoughts, disarmed by the loving tenderness with which she set forth stern unbending truths, young men could not but acknowledge her right to a hearing. Bombay has lost one of its best speakers to young men; the Christian Church, one of the noblest of its workers."

A Brahmin Pandit, not a Christian, who served under Mrs Fuller in translation work, and in the tuition of Alliance missionaries in Marathi, wrote: "She was one of the few persons who could reach the hearts of the people of this country, and consider themselves as one of them. . . . Wherever she went, either among educated or uneducated classes of the people, she was liked by all. The one quality that made her so, was the deep and real interest she showed and felt for the people. Her heart was full of love for them. . . . She also fully understood how to touch others at the point of sympathy. This does not mean that she would shrink from being at issue with anybody on account of her opinions. She had independent thoughts, and was courageous enough to give out her convictions, but I always marked that she never forced me at the start to put myself over against her for a contest. This is the secret of influencing others to see as we do."

Mr Malabari, a non-Christian social reformer in Bombay, writing in his paper, the *Indian Spectator*, made a note on her death which illustrates what the above writer states, as to her method of meeting everybody at the point of sympathy. Mr Malabari wrote: "Never was the proximity of a great historical movement brought home more forcibly than when Mrs Fuller said that she had, as a child, met William Lloyd Garrison on his visits to her parents. 'Except ye become . . . as little children,' said the Master, pointing to a group of children, 'ye shall not enter into the Kingdom of Heaven.' Mrs Fuller lived up to the precept. She was a truly Christian woman, with a faith in her Saviour that was very touching. She threw herself, heart and soul, into her work, for the orphans especially, and lived for it. Not a few, who were neither of her race nor creed, will miss the kindly presence and earnest conversation of the deceased lady."

These extracts give the clue to why Mrs Fuller was, as the *Bombay Guardian* said, "the best known woman missionary in Western India, and the best loved."

APPENDIX

I. TESTIMONIES FROM FAR AND NEAR

SYMPATHISING letters poured in when it was known that the Home call had released the dear sufferer from the bonds of earth and flesh. The One Spirit sought to pour comfort into the wounded and bereaved heart of her husband by a multitude of earthly channels. No formal condolences these. The joy to which *she* had attained ; the blank her absence would be to her friends ; the power of the Lord to comfort and heal, and personal testimonies of blessing received through the life so lived for God, was the burden of their message, whether they came from friends throughout India, America, or even from China. The following extracts are selected as showing what the influence was that made her removal so widely felt. They are testimonies from outsiders, members of many different denominations ; none of the writers in this section being connected with the Christian Alliance.

FROM MISSIONARIES IN INDIA

"It is more than twenty-one years since I first met your dear wife. We often did not meet for quite an interval, but each time I found her ever the same, so loving and so sweet. . . . I do praise God for all He did through her. Surely some of us will be stimulated the more to serve Him, because He has taken her home."—C. S. P., *Bombay.*

"Surely the people of India have lost in her one of their sincerest friends. And yet, somehow, the word 'lost' seems out of place. May we not at least hope that in some way her influence is still going forth on their behalf. Hers was no ordinary missionary's life and work. She not only worked for the heathen herself, but her sweet simple life was a continual inspiration to other missionaries to be more wholly devoted. . . . When we gathered at 'Berachah' on Thursday, my one cry to God was that He would enable me to live closer to Him, and be more devoted to His service."—T. A. B., *Bombay.*

"What a blessed testimony she has left behind her! I know many will praise God for the example of her wholly consecrated and devoted life."—C. D. G., *Bombay.*

"Those few times I heard dear Mrs Fuller speak are deeply impressed on heart and memory. I feel I have personally lost a most kind friend; and in her zeal and love for the Master may I have grace so to follow her good example."—G. H. H., *Bombay*.

"She is at Home, and we shall soon be there; in the meantime I praise God for the inspiration her holy consistent life has been to me. It has many times been an object lesson to see how she humbled herself under God's hands, and let herself be disciplined by Him in the trials and difficulties that came to her. I am sure that many are to-day blessed and useful workers in His vineyard, owing to the way she laboured in prayer and believed for them till they came out into rest and victory. She was a true mother in Israel; may we follow her as she followed Christ. We know that more than ever your sufficiency will be of GOD, who will not fail you, but *is* enabling you to glorify Him. In view of the Lord's near coming, who can tell how much all this means."—H. R.,[1] *Bombay*.

"I praise God I ever knew her. May we seek to live as truly for God as she did. She had this testimony that she pleased God. Almost

[1] Helen Richardson passed within the veil one year after Mrs Fuller.

the last talk we had together before I left Bombay, speaking of Miss Park, she said: 'I envy her. Oh, it will be lovely to get Home.' There was a longing in her tone that made me feel how truly she looked forward to that time."—L. L., *Rangoon*.

"I owe very much to dear Mrs Fuller's counsel, and her sympathy at all times. Whenever I saw her I saw some manifestation of the life of the Master, His humility and selflessness and kindness."—M. W. M., *Poona*.

"We will push on with the work she has left, devoting ourselves yet more fully to God. It seems so strange that God should take one so well fitted for work, and doing it so well. But He will help us who are left to carry on the great work in His name and strength. We are filled with sorrow for you, but rejoice for our glorified sister."—D. O. and E. W. F., *Poona*.

"From the time your wife first came to our home in Ellichpur at the beginning of 1877, we have felt an interest in her perhaps greater than in any other servant of the Lord with whom we were permitted to have fellowship. And now she has gone to her exceeding great reward! I feel that in departing she could say as but few of Christ's servants in these days could: 'I have fought a good fight; I have finished my course; I have kept the faith. Henceforth there is laid up for me a crown of righteousness!' May God help us all to follow her as she followed the Master."—A. N., *Dhond.*

"The world will to very many of us seem for ever the poorer for the loss of one who was indeed a power wherever she went."—M. T., *Ahmedabad.*

"Mrs Fuller will be much missed by all who knew her in this and other lands. I thank God I had the privilege of making her acquaintance personally last year, as I had before done by reading articles from her pen. Her articles on Indian womanhood I read with great interest and profit."—J. J., *Sangli.*

"We have just been studying in Romans ix. of the sovereignty of God, and this seemed to come to show us that His way is beyond our ken, that He will not have us lay down any laws for Him. We can only say: 'Lo these are parts of His ways.' Some day we will be able to read the other side. What an abundant entrance she must have had. I do hope God's people will give Him alone the glory for all the answers to prayer which He has granted in the past three months of illness, and all her life long."—M. H., *Kodaikanal.*

"We had hoped that God would spare her to you and to us and to many others. But He required her elsewhere, her training was complete, and so she was transferred to higher service. We are still at college, but she has graduated and passed out, or rather passed in."—R. J. W., *Coonoor.*

"Mrs Fuller has been a great blessing to my soul. I was always glad to meet her. Her visit to us at Sanand was a great blessing to me."—A. S., *Coonoor.*

OTHER FRIENDS IN INDIA

"I cannot refrain from writing to express the very sincere regret that I feel at the loss to you and to your children and the Christian Church of one so earnest and so taught of God. I had the great pleasure of meeting your wife at my cousin's house in Bombay when she was Miss Frow. . . . I have ever had the encouraging recollection of Miss Frow's faith in God at that time. The remembrance of her trust in Christ is a great savour."—G. W., *Murree.*

"The loss is not yours only, but one in which many will share, and will sorrow not only out of sympathy with you, but from a sense of personal bereavement."—G. C. W., *Bangalore.*

"Eternity will alone reveal the worth and fragrance of the beautiful Christ-life lived by dear Mrs Fuller. And how many poor Indian Christians are personally poorer by her translation. I cried as though I had lost my very own sister of flesh and blood on hearing the news. Never did I meet or have a few words with her but with an uplifting influence and effect. Thanks be unto God for such a life. Words are poor comforters. It is only 'Till He come.'"—F. L. R., *Bangalore.*

"The loss was not yours only, it was such a loss to the world. My wife wants to see you to get from you, if you have it, the MSS. of Mrs Fuller's life of Mr Finney [in Marathi]. She had begun it several years ago. I translated some chapters, too. If you do not find the MSS. send me the book from which Mrs Fuller was writing the Life. I will translate such portions as I think fit, in memory of the dear sister."—S. R. M., *Ahmednagar.*

TESTIMONY FROM WESTERN LANDS

"What a perfect benediction her life was. She was an ideal Gospel Christian, rejoicing in the true sense always, and giving God thanks from the depths of her heart. I count it one of the rare privileges of my life to have seen and known her as I did. She has been a great spiritual help to me. Eternity alone will reveal what the Lord has wrought through her perfectly yielded spirit to His will."—C. F. H., *Brooklyn.*

"So powerful was her influence that even the great distance that was so much of the time between us did not seem to me to separate us. Truly she was one of the most beloved of our Blessed Master's disciples, one of the dearest to our Father's heart of all His children. A martyr's glorious reward is hers."—S. P. K., *New York.*

"Sister Fuller was such an institution in Bombay. Her cheery, kind presence, and above all her very spiritual and instructive addresses will be greatly missed. This applies to all the churches, for she was welcome in all our circles, and as a worker seemed one who could ill be spared."—J. M., *London.*

"The fragrance of her memory will live long, not only through her kindly deeds and loving helpful words, but her pen will enable her to speak to the hearts of friends and strangers, and will, as the years go by, bring many to Jesus."—J. K. T., *Toronto.*

"She was a remarkable woman, especially suited for the work of a missionary. Her gifts were great and her wisdom to guide and suggest equally so. She had much power as a writer. I always stopped to read all over her signature, and never was disappointed in its interest. But more than all was her entire consecration and sweet personality."—S. E. O., *New York.*

"We remember her kindly words, her earnest faith and the immeasurable zeal and love for the Master's work she so continually manifested."—G. P. T., *Paterson, New Jersey.*

"Not many deaths, so far as I can now recall, outside of our own family circle, have affected my wife so deeply as this bereavement. She had learned to love Sister Fuller dearly, and she appreciated her character in all of its various aspects. I had known her for many years, and it is perhaps the highest praise I could give her to say that in all my recollections of her the most prominent feature has been her Christian character."—Bishop J. M. Thoburn, *Lake Bluff, Ill.*

"As I wrote in an article which will appear

in *The Christian Herald* next week, so I say now: That as Mrs Fuller went up and into the presence of her Lord, her first petition was for the dear people for whose conversion from darkness to light, and from death to life, she consecrated her talents, her time, her life. My only regret is that when we met at your house and she was ill in an adjoining room, that I did not press more urgently my desire to see her—and yet, perhaps, it is best as it is."—Dr LOUIS KLOPSCH, Proprietor, New York *Christian Herald*.

"About the same time, the week your beloved one fell asleep, we were called out by the Spirit here in our Prayer Union to unite for a week together in prayer for you and yours. We know God heard and answered and all is well. It will be a great sorrow to many who hear of your bereavement, but this sorrow will be made to abound most fruitfully as we look toward the fulfilling of the Blessed Hope.

"I had long thought of writing to you and Sister Fuller about an article she published in the spring or early summer of 1894 on "The Ministry of Prayer." The Lord used it to call me to this ministry which has resulted in the PENTECOSTAL PRAYER UNION, the influence of which is reaching out increasingly into all the earth. The fruits of it here in

Los Angelos can never be estimated. Only yesterday there came into my hand an address delivered before the Ministerial Union of the Presbyterian Church of San Francisco, which address is one of the most remarkable on the subject I have ever seen. This had its spring in the work last winter in this city—and all had its rise in that call through Sister Fuller in 1894. I have often borne testimony to this, and I pray that God will multiply it."—H. C. WADDELL, Editor of *Prayer, Los Angelos, California.*

II. FROM ALLIANCE MISSIONARIES IN INDIA

MRS JESSIE SIMMONS

How we miss our dear Sister Fuller. Loving service was the keynote of her life. All her unusual gifts of mind and heart were at the service of others. Both in our mission homes and in the work at large her chief aim in life was to be a humble instrument in God's hands to be used of Him freely. To my knowledge she never made her weakness of body an excuse for refusing work of any kind which she believed was sent of God. She knew the blessed secret of taking life from Jesus day by day, and was a testimony to God's keeping power.

Her faith in God was mighty, and her keen and wise insight and forethought in matters concerning our work made her an invaluable counsellor. She was always reaching out for even wider lines of usefulness, and being a clear thinker and able writer, she translated and wrote many valuable books. She lived an unselfish life, and was always happiest when she saw others reaching out and growing in grace.

Her love for the native Christians was marvellous. She longed to see a real outpouring of the Holy Spirit upon them, realising how much God could use them among their own people. This was the burden of her prayer; may ours be the re-echo of it.

We know not why God has taken such an able and useful life. But we bow our heads and say "Thy will be done," and cry out for her mantle to fall upon us.

Mrs Carrie Bates Rogers

My husband and I went to see her near the beginning of her last illness. She could scarcely speak above a whisper, and that with difficulty. Her first words to us were inquiries as to what we were to do for the hot season, and hoping we should be comfortable.

Later on, when we brought her to our temporary home at Igatpuri, in the intervals between her times of physical anguish, her mind would go out as usual to the dear missionaries and their needs in those famine days, and she would try to plan ways by which she hoped one and another might be able to get away from their stations for a little change and rest.

She had a dainty doll's cot, with furnishings, which she wished our little girls to have. She had it brought to her that she might personally see that all was in spotless order, and took keen delight in thinking of the pleasure it would afford them.

She had a rare gift of clear, forcible exposition of Scripture, always weaving in so much of heart experience that her teachings went from her own heart down deep into the hearts of her hearers. How we miss her, words cannot express. "Her works do follow her."

Mrs Martha Ramsey

Our first meeting with dear Mrs Fuller was after the Board had accepted us for India in 1892, when, in the Berachah Home parlour, New York, she advised us as to outfits, etc. Her simple motherly way drew us to her at once, and her frankness in every detail of the conversation gave us respect for her. . . . These two qualities ever seemed to us to characterise her, and we say with gratitude this love and respect never lessened one whit, and now that she is gone, they are only increased by many precious memories of her thoughtfulness and wise counsel.

During that interview we in our zeal expressed our longing to reach the women of India with the Gospel message, and we have never forgotten the answer, "When you get there they won't want you." In her talks to intending missionaries she avoided the sensational, and always held a high standard of motive; in fact, at times her faithfulness would almost seem to discourage, but we have praised God again and again since being on the field, and meeting with the difficulties, that she was so true.

Her presence on the voyage from London was a blessing. Often weak in body, but drawing strength from the Lord, she never failed both in the daily Bible-readings and in her walk and conversation, to inspire our little party with fresh determination to be true in the service to which God had called us, and also with rejoicing in the hope of the Second Coming of our blessed Redeemer.

How much we owe to her under God for help in every way as young missionaries, and in the language! She did for us what no Brahmin pundit would have known how to do. We remember how, standing out of sight, as we recited with the teacher, she would get to know our difficulties, and set to solving them at the first opportunity, but in such a kind way that one hardly knew till it was done. Later on, after little Robbie "fell asleep" (as she used to say), she took us all in a class, and helped us out of our difficulties in Marathi.

Her interest in each one individually was always so kindly expressed; forgetful of herself she would plan for others as if they were her own children. A visit from her was always looked forward to with pleasure, and the savour of the teaching she would give from God's Word lingered long after she had left us, not that she always said sweet things, for she was faithful to show us our faults and mistakes.

We have seen her on her face in prayer more than once for guidance or victory along a certain line. The last time but one in our home, God, in answer to her effectual fervent prayer, raised up a beloved sister from what seemed almost the gates of death, to take the journey to Bombay, and from that time it was victory to that dear one; but no one would have known who had not seen the wrestling in prayer, that dear Mrs Fuller was more than ordinarily exercised; then on the journey she spent much of the night on her face in prayer, and God preciously answered.

Her last visit to us was less than two months before her illness began, when she was *so* interested in the famine work, and so anxious lest we fall short of God's thought for the people. One of her messages then was that as Moses was as God to the Israelites, so we were to be at this time to those whom God would call out for His Name. Her favourite hymn just then was :—

> "Taking life from Jesus,
> Freely day by day,
> * * *
> Life and strength receiving,
> All our pilgrim way."

This she was literally doing—taking life step by step.

At her request I accompanied her to Buldana, a station twenty-eight miles off the railway, and I shall always be thankful for the experience of that journey with her. The seats on the mail tonga were engaged, and it didn't seem as if we could get bullocks for that day. She longed to go home, for she was tired, but felt God wanted her to go and see the dear missionaries at Buldana, so in answer to prayer the bullocks came, and we started off late in the afternoon, hoping to reach our destination about midnight. However, as so often is the case, there was difficulty in getting change of bullocks at the different stages, notwithstanding that a friend of Mrs Fuller's, a Christian Government official, had sent his servant all the way to help; so it was past four in the morning when we arrived at the bungalow. Not one word of complaint passed her lips, nothing but praise to God all the way, and as she paid the different drivers, she *always* gave as much over the Government rates as would make up for the extra price of fodder in the scarcity, but gave it in such a way that the man would be encouraged, and not as a charity.

Her shawl was heavier than mine and the night was bitterly cold, so she cunningly said, "Your shawl is smooth and mine is rough, and I don't like it so well. Let me take yours," just that I might be comfortable.

She was needed in Bombay, so began the return journey that same afternoon on the mail tonga. That was the last time we saw her in health.

Before her Home-going I was privileged to spend a few days with her, and although in pain and weakness she still had the same love for the work and the missionaries, and would speak of both again and again.

It did seem as if she was needed here, but God knew best, and as she said one day, "If I am to go, you dear ones must just take it that my work is finished."

We miss her, oh, so much, and often long for her counsel and her prayers, but would not call her back if we might, for her work here *was* finished, but *there* "His servants shall serve Him," and still she "being dead yet speaketh."

Mrs Blanche Hamilton

Although labouring for many years in Berar, India, and being specially called to work among the Marathi people, yet no one felt more an interest or burden for the work in Gujarat than she. Six years ago a party of eleven entered Gujarat when the Alliance work was new, and it would be hard to tell how much her prayers and occasional visits to this field meant to us and to the people. What a help she was in every way in all the trials accompanying pioneering—learning a new language, becoming accustomed to the people and their ways, with no one of the party experienced—may never be fully known.

Since called to her reward, many of her earnest prayers and steps taken by faith for the work in Gujarat have been realised. During one visit to this field, God seemed to give her an enlarged vision for the work, and she was so impressed by it that she called us all together and gave it under the beautiful Bible lesson of Ezekiel's river vision. Although at the time there was not one convert, she seemed to see the work spreading and reaching out over a long strip of country down to the sea. It seemed so impossible, but we have watched God's plans unfolding until we have seen that vision fulfilled. The first to come into the light was a poor woman who was covered with sores and at times was possessed of a devil. The evil spirit was cast out—and she was partially restored to health, and later on her face used to light up with joy on hearing Jesus' name. The Christians now number about 400, besides a girls' orphanage of 360, and one for boys at Dholka numbering about 400.

In trying to recall some of the many touching incidents that time fails to erase, it seems as if she could not have been more one with us; she shared our joys and sorrows in such a measure that her departure seemed like a great prop being removed. It is impossible to say enough of her loving, tender sympathy. One afternoon while busy with the study of the language, things began to grow dark, and before night dear Miss Montgomery and myself were down with cholera. We felt so much the need of her prayers that a telegram was sent immediately to Berachah Home, Bombay, and instead of simply praying for us there, she left at once for Gujarat. Soon after her arrival she gave a Bible-reading that brought fresh courage, and later on deliverance; my life was spared for further years of precious service. Miss M. was called to a higher service above, and a touching little incident transpired as she was being carried out of the compound for interment in Bishop Heber's churchyard. A crowd of native women came over weeping from the camp near by; although not able to speak Gujarati, yet, as always, Mrs Fuller could not refrain from turning everything to God's glory. She talked to them of heaven (through an interpreter) with such earnestness that to this day, six years later, they often speak of it. It was literally true that she "sowed beside all waters."

When the famine began in Gujarat she was still one of the first to advise and help. Many were the messages of power given to the women, and she understood their need and hearts as few do. Having to talk through an interpreter she at last began to study Gujarati. Her efforts were untiring, though her other labours were great, and we rejoiced to think she would soon be able to give our women some of her loving messages of power in the vernacular, but ere the time came she was transplanted to a higher realm and sphere, while we here below learn from those she has helped and influenced that her works still continue.

III. IN MEMORIAM

By Miss HATTIE L. BRUCE, American Marathi Misson, Satara

"IN this life of faith in the natural, and disinclination to the supernatural, we want especially to meet the whole world with this *credo*, 'I believe in the Holy Ghost.'"

These words, though written by another, seem always associated in my mind with Mrs Fuller, because she it was from whom I caught their spirit, years ago. "Do you believe in the Holy Ghost?" I never shall forget the circumstances under which she asked me this question, after a refusal on my part to address a large children's gathering at our annual *Sabha*. She, being like a mother to me in things spiritual, had taken me very seriously to task for my refusal. All excuses—that I was not free in Marathi, that I had had no time for preparation, that another could do far better than I—she simply brushed aside with the words, "If you believe in the Holy Ghost, you will speak to-morrow." And my pleadings to the contrary were in vain, though with hands clasped, and almost on my knees before her, I lingered till eleven o'clock that night, in hopes that she would relent. She knew me to be in a position where I had no alternative but to obey, and she took advantage of it to make me venture out upon God. This is only one illustration of how she pushed me into deep water. I had given her the right to do so, for, as said above, she was like a mother to me. Besides, in early days, her longings and definite choice had been, like mine, for the supernatural, and all through life she had proven the "God of impossibilities." As I longed to prove Him, I could not but follow such a venturesome spirit, one who would go to all lengths with God. And so she led me on and on. "*Let God be true!*" How can I ever thank her for sharing with me the inspiration of her life!

I was always welcome in Mrs Fuller's home. "Come whenever you will, and bring your friends with you, only give me twenty-four hours' notice," she used to say, and many a time, both in Akola and Bombay, I have taken her at her word. Many are the heart to heart talks I have had with her. I would watch my opportunity to sit at her feet—all the better if it were evening, and the lights turned low—for then I could ask her to tell me what she saw to be wrong in my life. Was she not my spiritual *confidante*? In her inimitable way she would perhaps begin: "You want me to size you up? Well, I think you're lovely!"

And then she would go on to show me the reverse! "The truth in love"—it was not hard to hear it from her lips.

Once during a season of special meetings which Mrs Fuller conducted at Mahableshwar, she was my guest. What happy times we had together in our little grass *chupper*! She was the only friend who ever thought it worth while to give "Bible-readings for one," to me alone. But I could not have her all to myself even after her day's work seemed done, for there were so many missionaries who made appointments to meet and talk with her, that she was sometimes kept up at night. With that delightful humour of hers, she remarked to me one evening: "I'm afraid you'll be put out by what I've done!" "Do you think it's so easy to put me out?" I asked. "I mean put out physically," she answered. "Miss —— wanted a talk with me, and I couldn't arrange for it in any other way than to offer her your bed. You don't mind going over to her place to sleep to-night, do you?" So this is how Mrs Fuller "put me out"—out of my own house, out of my own bed—and I loved her the more for it! She was made a great blessing to the dear ones at Mahableshwar that season. One of them confessed to me, "She helps by her life, by her presence, more than by anything she says." But her words, too, were spoken in the power of the Spirit, and many of us will treasure them as long as we live. "I am not a teacher," she said to me once; "God only gives me sweet thoughts."

I never shall forget the call we made together upon a stranger who showed herself wholly out of sympathy with us and our work. Mrs Fuller remarked afterwards, "Didn't she snub me, though? I tell you, there's one thing the devil can't imitate, and that is *the sweetness of Jesus!*" With the very sweetness of Jesus she had herself learned to meet the rejection, the misunderstandings and the trials of her lot. "I belong to a kingdom that is yet to come," she once simply replied, when asked her nationality; and all her life witnessed to her being a pilgrim, a stranger here. How she pleaded, "Thy Kingdom come!" How abundant was she in labours for the salvation of the people, "Marathi salvation," as she used to call it, adding sometimes, "I do not want long life unless God shows me His salvation!" (Ps. xci. 16). More than all, how her heart was set upon Jesus' coming again! "*Till he come!*" Dear heart, so weary with love and longing, it will not be hard to wait now.

"For so He giveth His beloved sleep."

By Mrs F. Percy Horne, of the *Bombay Guardian*

The first time I saw Mrs Fuller was at an evening service in the spacious Grant Road Methodist Church in Bombay. She had just returned from America with a large party of missionaries for the then new Alliance Mission, and had been asked to give the address in place of a sermon. Her words came with power, and the subject of the address has never passed from my memory. She spoke of the power of Christ in the heart in contrast to the doctrine of "perfection," and she told how at one time she believed she had received the blessing of "a clean heart," but she looked at her heart and examined her feelings so closely that her eyes were turned away from Jesus. But later He had taught her the rest of allowing Him to dwell in her heart. *Now* the difficulty of loving those whom she naturally did not love was gone, now the difficulty of speaking was over, and now the irksomeness of work was past. Jesus loved through her; He spoke through her; and He worked through her; and she gladly acquiesced. Later, when I knew her more intimately, I found that her words were true. Her life was an outward testimony of the indwelling Christ.

When the entire work of this office devolved

on us we had no kinder friend. Nearly every morning when she was in Bombay she would come in for a few minutes' "gup," and sometimes we shared the "sweet message" the Lord had given her that morning. And often she would write it down for a larger circle, for the pages of the *Guardian.* She often made me think of the words, "There is that scattereth and yet increaseth" — she gave lavishly of her talent, her love, and her sunny kindness, and all these gifts were abundantly replenished.

Ours was only one of the households she visited in Bombay, but we felt she belonged to us. What a number of little joys she brought! Sometimes it was a charming letter from her daughter in America; another time a pretty photograph; once a plate of some strawberries which had been brought for her from the hills. The last gift was some lovely pinks which a friend had brought for her from Panchgani. Mr Fuller wrote a day or two before the call came: "She picked out a part of them with her own hand, and asked that they be sent to you with her love. She is no better, humanly speaking, but twelve weeks ago yesterday she seemed nearer death than now, and the doctor said she would not live till morning. She has been all these weeks like the burning bush—burning but not consumed."

When the call came and the news spread over the city, a large concourse of people gathered at Berachah Home. It was the saddest funeral I ever attended; missionaries from all the mission houses were present, and Indian Christians of all ranks crowded the entry and the passages. Our workmen begged an hour's leave to take farewell of the body of one who had endeared herself to them by innumerable acts of kindness. I remember how after the brief service, and when the triumphant singing was stilled, a hush fell upon the assembly that was almost painful. The stillness was so tense that it was a relief when a child's cry broke it, and then the tears of the women flowed freely as they filed round the casket. The grief of the native Christians was intense; she made herself one with them; I never knew a missionary to understand them better. Mrs Fuller could make an Indian do anything she wished. I remember how our *mali* (gardener) would do his utmost to obtain cuttings of the plants she desired for her garden; I remember, too, that we hardly ever went into her house without meeting some Indian Christian who had gone to her for advice or help. She was no respecter of persons, unless it were that she sought out and devoted herself to those who most needed her help.

IV. COVENANT PROMISES TO PARENTS

A BIBLE READING BY MRS FULLER

HOW many parents there are whose one great burden is their children. Many of them are selfish in this, because it is *their* children, and it would be so nice to have them saved, and be good, and go to church with them, and never have any bad habits. They are interested in no one else's children. But there are parents whose motives are not selfish, who pray and shed many tears, but always seem at sea for any definite promise to lay hold of for their children. I have had many parents beg me to pray for their children, and when I have asked them, "Do you believe and plead the covenant promises for them?" I have found many who did not know what they were.

God says, "Lo, children are an heritage of the Lord: and the fruit of the womb is His reward" (Ps. cxxvii. 3). If this is true, He has made provision for them.

God made

A WONDERFUL COVENANT

with Abraham. In him it was wonderfully fulfilled: "I will . . . be a God unto thee, and to thy seed after thee" (Gen. xvii. 7). The one brief condition for the fulfilment of this great promise was indicated by God when He said of Abraham: "I know him, that he will command his children and his household after him, and they shall keep the way of the Lord, to do justice and judgment, that the Lord may bring upon Abraham that which He hath spoken of him" (Gen. xviii. 19).

To ratify this, God gave to Abraham the usual token of a covenant between two parties. The word covenant means "a cutting." The animal for sacrifice was cut in two, and the covenanting party passed between the pieces. In Gen. xv. we read of how God, the covenanting party, sealed His pledge to Abraham. A lamp of fire passed between the pieces, and thus God identified Himself with Abraham and his seed. "For the first time since man left the gate of the garden of Eden, there appeared the symbol of the glory of God which was afterward to shine in the pillar of cloud and the Shekinah gleam." He could swear by no greater, so he swore by Himself, "I will . . . be a God to thee and to thy seed after thee."

"Abraham believed God, and it was counted unto him for righteousness" (Gen. xv. 6; Rom. iv. 3).

But it was never God's thought that the Hebrews should live for themselves or to themselves.

HE EXPANDS HIS THOUGHT—

"In thee shall all the families of the earth be blessed." And it is His thought for us still. "I will bless thee . . . and thou shalt be a blessing" (Gen. xii. 2).

And now, dear fathers and mothers, "If ye be Christ's, then are ye Abraham's seed and

HEIRS ACCORDING TO THE PROMISE"

(Gal. iii. 29). God will be a "God unto thee and to thv seed after thee." We believe this covenant includes us all. "God pledges Himself to be the God of our seed, but it is for us to claim the fulfilment of His pledge. Not in heart-rending cries, but in quiet determined faith, let us ask Him to do as He said." Let us "also walk in the steps of that faith of our father Abraham, which he had" (Rom. iv. 12).

Let us turn to the first great covenant promise which is the key-note to all the rest. "And I will establish My covenant between Me and thee and thy seed after thee, in their generations, for an everlasting covenant, to be a God unto thee, and to thy seed after thee" (Gen. xvii. 7). Over and over in the Old Testament is this thought repeated in different dress.

Deut. xii. 28. "Observe and hear all these words which I command thee, that it may go well with thee, and with thy children after thee for ever."

Deut. xi. 18-21. "Lay up these My words in your heart . . . and ye shall teach them your children . . . that your days may be multiplied and the days of your children . . . as the days of heaven upon the earth." How little long life for ourselves or for our children is to be desired unless our and their days can be "as the days of heaven upon the earth."

Ps. ciii. 17, 18. David reiterates the thought. "But the mercy of the Lord is from everlasting to everlasting upon them that fear Him, and His righteousness unto children's children; to such as keep His covenant, and to those that remember His commandments to do them."

Isa. xliv. 3. Isaiah gives some most precious promises: "I will pour My Spirit upon thy seed, and My blessing upon thine offspring." Let us couple that with Peter's declaration on the Day of Pentecost: "And

THE PROMISE IS UNTO YOU, AND TO YOUR CHILDREN"

(Acts ii. 39), and press boldly to the throne of grace that our children as well as ourselves shall possess this gift of the Holy Ghost.

Isa. liv. 13. "And all thy children shall be

taught of the Lord ; and great shall be the peace of thy children." How often the Spirit has applied this promise to the heart of a praying parent.

Isa. lix. 21 comes to us with all the solemnity of an oath or covenant : "My Spirit that is upon thee, and My words which I have put in thy mouth, shall not depart out of thy mouth, nor out of the mouth of thy seed, nor out of the mouth of thy seed's seed, saith the Lord, from henceforth and for ever." Of the great grandmother of Fidelia Fiske it is written : "Her last days were days of almost continued praying : and the burden of her prayer then was, as it had previously been, that her posterity might be a godly seed even to the latest generation." Of her, Miss Fiske writes to a cousin : "Have you heard your father tell how she used to pray for her descendants to the end of time?" In 1857 three hundred of the descendants of this godly woman were members of Christ's Church. Miss Fiske adds in speaking of it : "I often think I may be receiving blessing in answer to her prayers : for I know that she prayed for her children's children for all coming time." This was a grasping of the promise, for "thy seed's seed." On the opening page of Miss Fiske's life it says : "Fidelia Fiske was a child of the covenant." Precious record.

Mr Hastings tells of a father and mother

who set apart an hour every Sabbath morning to pray for their children. They were all converted, and as they grew up and had families, they followed their parents' custom of prayer: so that at the time of writing the sketch, there had been four generations of this godly pair, and not one out of the four generations had ever been known to die unsaved. A number were ministers of the Gospel and missionaries and otherwise useful men and women.

Jer. xxxii. 39 says: "I will give them one heart, and one way, that they may fear Me for ever, for the good of them, *and of their children after them.*"

Deuteronomy xxx. 6 brings a precious promise to claim: "And the Lord thy God will circumcise thine heart, and the heart of thy seed, to love the Lord thy God with all thine heart, and with all thy soul, that thou mayest live." Dear parent, as you have realised that God was circumcising your heart to love Him more fully, has it never given you power to get down on your knees and claim the same for your children? To spiritually apprehend this gives a parent great boldness to approach God for his family.

FOR CHRISTIANS AS WELL AS FOR JEWS.

But some may say: "Oh, these promises are good enough, but they are all for the

Jews." It seems to us that God could give no greater denial to this than when Peter so boldly on the day of Pentecost, at the beginning of the new dispensation, gave God's thought for the family anew, as he said: "For the promise is unto you, *and to your children*" (Acts ii. 39). Can it not be said of many: "Ye have not, because ye ask not"? The Holy Ghost bade Peter also tell Cornelius words whereby he *and all his house should be saved* (Acts xi. 14). And when the Philippian jailor cried out, "What must I do to be saved?" Paul replied: "Believe on the Lord Jesus Christ, and thou shalt be saved, *and thy house.*"

I fear that we missionaries have not always been true to the people of India in giving them the Gospel. We have over and over exhorted them to "Believe on the Lord Jesus Christ, and thou shalt be saved"; and then have stopped there. But in a land where a man has to cut every sacred tie to become a follower of Jesus, and literally forsake parents, wife, and often children, we should go on to the end of the verse and add—"*and thy house.*" Family ties make one of the greatest hindrances convicted souls in India have in confessing Jesus. We believe if this promise could be flashed into their hearts by the Holy Ghost, as the living word of God, that the life it would bring would give power to step out, and courage to go back to their friends and tell them what God has done for them, and it would give them faith to labour to bring their friends to Christ amidst persecution and perhaps even to martyrdom. "And thy house."

Some may say: "I know so many good people of whom this is not true of their children." "Let God be true, but every man a liar" (Rom. iii. 4). Perhaps they never believed these promises. The Bible is full of promises of the baptism of the Spirit, but how many good people never receive it. And when one does receive it, he sees he might have been filled long before if he had but comprehended and laid hold of God's promises. These promises are given to parents of a certain character, and as parents believe, their power to command their house (Gen xviii. 19), and a faithfulness to teach (Deut. xi. 18) their children, as they could not otherwise have done, is given.

Others may say, "My children have long got the start of me," or "I did not know God or care when I was with my children, and they have long gone from under my influence." We know nothing to do but to humble ourselves to God, and confess it all: and confess it to the children, and then bring the promises to God.

Another may say: "But my husband, or

my wife is not a Christian, what can I do?" God seems not to have forgotten such cases. Turn to 1 Cor. vii. 14. The case is more easily understood in heathen lands where there are different religions. Mr Coles says, "'holy' and 'unclean' must be certainly taken in the putative sense, *i.e.* the children are nominally Christian, not pagan: the family becomes a Christian household by the Christianity of either parent. Whatever prerogatives belong to the Christian family accrue to this by virtue of the faith of either parent. I see no reason to doubt that Paul had distinctly in mind the covenant relation which Christian households sustain to God in reference to the consecration of their offspring under the great promise: 'I will be a God to thee and to thy seed after thee.' Paul interprets this covenant to apply to 'thee' in cases where only one of the parents is a believer. Most tenderly and mercifully God provides that the personal faith of either parent shall be honoured as sufficient ground to claim all the promises of this most precious covenant."

The Spirit, too, in a time of prayer may apply a promise to our hearts of a verse we had never thought of in this connection. A widow was once greatly exercised in prayer for her children. The Spirit applied with power to her the words: "Leave thy fatherless children with Me, and I will preserve them alive." She rested her heart, and they were all converted.

Turn to Heb. xi. "By faith Noah prepared an ark *to the saving of his house.*" Andrew Murray says: "The faith of Noah, made perfect by works, saved his family; and with his family he saved the race. The old story of 'I will bless thee and thou shalt be a blessing.'" He further adds: "*By faith Isaac blessed Jacob and Esau.* His blessing on his children was the manifestation of his faith in the promise of God to his father and himself, and the transmission of the blessiug to them. *By faith Jacob blessed each of the sons of Joseph.* . . . Faith was the secret inspiration of their treatment of their children. Faith never confines itself to the person of the believer himself, but takes in his home and children. And how is it that Christian parents can secure this longed-for-blessing for their children? There is but one answer. By faith. Our life must be all faith. The blessing and the power are His: and it is as we have more of God in our life and our home, there will be the hidden power resting on our children. Faith does not only mean a knowing that there is a covenant promise for our children, and a pleading of it in prayer. This is an exercise of faith and has great value. But the chief thing is the life; faith is the making way for God and giving Him place in our life. And when at times the vision tarries, and the promise appears to fail, faith understands this as only a call to trust God more completely and more confidently. As we hold fast our confidence firm to the end, as in patience and long-suffering we are strong in faith, giving glory to God, we shall know for certain that we shall inherit this promise too: 'I will . . . be a God to thee and to thy seed after thee.'"

But in closing remember, dear friends, that God never meant that just your family should be saved. God's word was to Abraham and it is to you: "*And in thee shall all the families of the earth be blessed.*" Let not your thought and prayer be: "My seed and my seed's seed"; but teach your children and give them to God that He may take them and make them a blessing to the nations of the earth.

May our children indeed be children of the covenant in its widest fulfilment. Amen.